Cloning

OPPOSING VIEWPOINTS®

Tamara L. Roleff, *Book Editor*

Bruce Glassman, *Vice President*
Bonnie Szumski, *Publisher*
Helen Cothran, *Managing Editor*

OPPOSING
VIEWPOINTS®
SERIES

GREENHAVEN PRESS
An imprint of Thomson Gale, a part of The Thomson Corporation

THOMSON
™
GALE

Detroit • New York • San Francisco • San Diego • New Haven, Conn.
Waterville, Maine • London • Munich

For more information, contact
Greenhaven Press
27500 Drake Rd.
Farmington Hills, MI 48331-3535
Or you can visit our Internet site at http://www.gale.com

LIBRARY OF CONGRESS CATALOGING-IN-PUBLICATION DATA
Cloning / Tamara L. Roleff, book editor.
p. cm. — (Opposing viewpoints)
Includes bibliographical references and index.
ISBN 0-7377-3311-X (lib. : alk. paper) — ISBN 0-7377-3312-8 (pbk. : alk. paper)
1. Cloning—Social aspects. I. Roleff, Tamara L., 1959– . II. Opposing viewpoints series (Unnumbered)
QH442.2.C5644 2006
176—dc22   2005046165

"Congress shall make
no law...abridging the
freedom of speech, or of
the press."

First Amendment to the U.S. Constitution

The basic foundation of our democracy is the First
Amendment guarantee of freedom of expression.
The Opposing Viewpoints Series is dedicated to the
concept of this basic freedom and the idea that it is
more important to practice it than to enshrine it.

Contents

Chapter 3: Should Researchers Use Adult or Embryonic Stem Cells?

Chapter 4: Should Cloning Be Banned?

Why Consider Opposing Viewpoints?

"The only way in which a human being can make some approach to knowing the whole of a subject is by hearing what can be said about it by persons of every variety of opinion and studying all modes in which it can be looked at by every character of mind. No wise man ever acquired his wisdom in any mode but this."

John Stuart Mill

In our media-intensive culture it is not difficult to find differing opinions. Thousands of newspapers and magazines and dozens of radio and television talk shows resound with differing points of view. The difficulty lies in deciding which opinion to agree with and which "experts" seem the most credible. The more inundated we become with differing opinions and claims, the more essential it is to hone critical reading and thinking skills to evaluate these ideas. Opposing Viewpoints books address this problem directly by presenting stimulating debates that can be used to enhance and teach these skills. The varied opinions contained in each book examine many different aspects of a single issue. While examining these conveniently edited opposing views, readers can develop critical thinking skills such as the ability to compare and contrast authors' credibility, facts, argumentation styles, use of persuasive techniques, and other stylistic tools. In short, the Opposing Viewpoints Series is an ideal way to attain the higher-level thinking and reading skills so essential in a culture of diverse and contradictory opinions.

In addition to providing a tool for critical thinking, Opposing Viewpoints books challenge readers to question their own strongly held opinions and assumptions. Most people form their opinions on the basis of upbringing, peer pressure, and personal, cultural, or professional bias. By reading carefully balanced opposing views, readers must directly confront new ideas as well as the opinions of those with whom they disagree. This is not to simplistically argue that everyone who reads opposing views will—or should— change his or her opinion. Instead, the series enhances readers' understanding of their own views by encouraging confrontation with opposing ideas. Careful examination of others' views can lead to the readers' understanding of the logical inconsistencies in their own opinions, perspective on why they hold an opinion, and the consideration of the possibility that their opinion requires further evaluation.

Evaluating Other Opinions

To ensure that this type of examination occurs, Opposing Viewpoints books present all types of opinions. Prominent spokespeople on different sides of each issue as well as well-known professionals from many disciplines challenge the reader. An additional goal of the series is to provide a forum for other, less known, or even unpopular viewpoints. The opinion of an ordinary person who has had to make the decision to cut off life support from a terminally ill relative, for example, may be just as valuable and provide just as much insight as a medical ethicist's professional opinion. The editors have two additional purposes in including these less known views. One, the editors encourage readers to respect others' opinions—even when not enhanced by professional credibility. It is only by reading or listening to and objectively evaluating others' ideas that one can determine whether they are worthy of consideration. Two, the inclusion of such viewpoints encourages the important critical thinking skill of objectively evaluating an author's credentials and bias. This evaluation will illuminate an author's reasons for taking a particular stance on an issue and will aid in readers' evaluation of the author's ideas.

It is our hope that these books will give readers a deeper understanding of the issues debated and an appreciation of the complexity of even seemingly simple issues when good and honest people disagree. This awareness is particularly important in a democratic society such as ours in which people enter into public debate to determine the common good. Those with whom one disagrees should not be regarded as enemies but rather as people whose views deserve careful examination and may shed light on one's own.

Thomas Jefferson once said that "difference of opinion leads to inquiry, and inquiry to truth." Jefferson, a broadly educated man, argued that "if a nation expects to be ignorant and free . . . it expects what never was and never will be." As individuals and as a nation, it is imperative that we consider the opinions of others and examine them with skill and discernment. The Opposing Viewpoints Series is intended to help readers achieve this goal.

David L. Bender and Bruno Leone,
Founders

Greenhaven Press anthologies primarily consist of previously published material taken from a variety of sources, including periodicals, books, scholarly journals, newspapers, government documents, and position papers from private and public organizations. These original sources are often edited for length and to ensure their accessibility for a young adult audience. The anthology editors also change the original titles of these works in order to clearly present the main thesis of each viewpoint and to explicitly indicate the opinion presented in the viewpoint. These alterations are made in consideration of both the reading and comprehension levels of a young adult audience. Every effort is made to ensure that Greenhaven Press accurately reflects the original intent of the authors included in this anthology.

Introduction

"Producing cloned babies would be desirable under certain circumstances, such as preventing genetic disease."
—Ian Wilmut, New Scientist, *February 21, 2004*

"[Genetic engineering of the human germline] could . . . open the door to human genetic enhancement for non-medical reasons."
—Donald Bruce, *"Problems with New Human Cloning Proposals," February 19, 2004*

Ian Wilmut, Keith Campbell, and their colleagues at the Roslin Institute in Scotland stunned the world in early 1997 when they announced that they had cloned a sheep, Dolly, from an udder cell of an adult ewe. The news was groundbreaking because Dolly was the first mammal to be cloned from an adult cell. All previous attempts at cloning had used embryonic cells. It is much more difficult to produce a clone using an adult cell than an embryonic cell because the adult cell has already become specialized; that is, it is a blood cell, or a nerve cell, or a skin cell. These specialized cells have lost their ability to change into other types of cells, whereas embryonic cells still have the capability to become any type of cell in the body.

Wilmut and his associates cloned Dolly by pioneering a new way of cloning adult cells, called somatic cell nuclear transplantation. They took a cell from the ewe's udder, removed the cell's nucleus, and then transplanted the nucleus into a sheep's egg cell that had had its nucleus removed. The two cells were then fused together with an electrical shock, which also started the process of cell division. The embryo was implanted in another sheep and allowed to gestate to maturity. Although Wilmut proved that an adult cell could be cloned, the process was fraught with difficulties; Dolly was the only sheep born in 277 attempts. Since Dolly's birth, numerous other mammals have been successfully cloned: goats, cats, mules, mice, and rabbits as well as exotic and endangered animals.

Wilmut and Campbell emphasized at the time of Dolly's announcement that they did not clone her with the intention of producing flocks of identical sheep. "Good old-fashioned sex," he said, was the best way to multiply sheep. Nor did he and his colleagues clone Dolly with the hope of cloning humans in the future. In fact, Wilmut admitted that he found the idea of human reproductive cloning repugnant and distasteful. But Wilmut has always maintained that cloning human embryos for therapeutic purposes could provide an important service to mankind. He claims that therapeutic cloning technology can be used to study inherited diseases, especially those that affect the heart or brain, such as Parkinson's or Lou Gehrig's disease. If a patient's embryonic stem cells can be recreated through cloning and coaxed into becoming motor neuron cells that are found in the brain, then scientists may be able to study the causes and progression of the patient's disease.

But the most promising development in human therapeutic cloning, according to Wilmut, would be repairing or curing genetic defects. For example, parents with genes for an inherited disease could create an embryo through in vitro fertilization technology. Scientists would remove the embryo's stem cells and correct the diseased gene using genetic engineering. Then the repaired stem cell's nucleus would be implanted into another egg cell. This embryo would be identical to the original embryo, Wilmut asserts; the only difference would be that the defective gene would have been corrected. The corrected embryo would then be implanted into the mother and allowed to develop into a healthy baby. The baby would be a clone not of one of its parents, but of the original embryo. "This form of cloning would not create the same ethical and social problems as reproductive cloning," Wilmut maintains. In fact, Wilmut proclaims, "cloning promises such great benefits that it would be immoral not to do it."

Not all agree with Wilmut's assessment of the ethical issues of therapeutic cloning. Donald Bruce, director of the Society, Religion, and Technology Project of the Church of Scotland, argues, "It is already highly controversial to advocate the use of cloned human embryos in research, but I am concerned that this new suggestion causes at least as many ethical problems as it might seem to solve." One of his biggest concerns is that repairing the stem cell's gene "amounts to genetic engineering of the human germline, in other words, it would make an irreversible change which was passed on to all future offspring." Such an action, he asserts, "is as ethically controversial as cloning itself, if not more so, in terms both of the risks and the ethics of permanently altering the genome of future generations." Bruce concludes that Wilmut's sweeping claim about the morality of therapeutic cloning is premature.

Other scientists, politicians, ethicists, commentators, and ordinary people oppose human cloning for additional reasons. Even if human cloning is used only for therapeutic procedures, cloning opponents argue that the dignity and sanctity of human life—even at its earliest embryonic stage—should prohibit the use of the technology. In a white paper on human cloning, the Florida Catholic Conference writes that it is opposed to human cloning because "many human embryos must be destroyed in the process; each of those failed trials involves the taking of an innocent human being. Each of the embryos has the capacity for developing into a full human." And according to commentator Wesley J. Smith, it is irrelevant if scientists say they only intend to use cloning technology for therapeutic treatments. "Unless society outlaws all human cloning," he writes in the *Weekly Standard*, "it is only a matter of time till the first cloned baby is on the way."

The first human has yet to be cloned, but it is clear that the danger and morality of the technology will be debated for some time to come. *Opposing Viewpoints: Cloning* examines the major arguments surrounding cloning and the related issue of stem cell research in the following chapters: Is Cloning Ethical? Can Therapeutic Cloning Cure Diseases? Should Researchers Use Adult or Embryonic Stem Cells? Should Cloning Be Banned? The potential benefits of cloning—and the safety and ethical issues involved—require that the implications be fully understood before the first human child is cloned.

CHAPTER 1

Is Cloning Ethical?

Chapter Preface

The public was forced to face the reality of cloning following the 1997 announcement that Dolly, a Finn Dorset sheep, had been cloned from a mammary cell of a six-year-old ewe. Since Dolly's arrival scientists around the world have cloned many different animals, including mice, cows, goats, pigs, rabbits, deer, a mule, a horse, and rare and endangered species such as mouflon, gaur, and banteng. Scientists chose to clone these animals for various reasons: Some were in danger of extinction; some offered characteristics advantageous to their species or to humans, such as disease resistance or high milk yield; some were transgenic animals (such as sheep or pigs that had human genes added to their DNA); and some were needed for research purposes. But in February 2002, researchers at Texas A&M University, in collaboration with a company named Genetics Savings & Clone (GSC), announced it had cloned the first pet, a cat named CC.

CC, short for Copycat, is not a carbon copy of its genetic donor. Rainbow, its genetic donor, is a brown, tan, and gold calico cat, whereas CC is a white-and-gray striped tabby. Genetic testing has proven, however, that CC is an identical twin to Rainbow. CC's coloring differs from Rainbow's due to a genetic anomaly that is unique to calico cats. Since CC's birth, five other pet owners have had their cats cloned by GSC—all in 2004—at a cost of $50,000 each: Tabouli and Baba Ganoush, Peaches, Nicky, and Gizmo. GSC has been unsuccessful so far in its attempts to clone a dog.

Animal welfare groups and other critics of cloning are alarmed about GSC cloning companion animals. They voice concerns about the safety of cloning and the suffering it causes to the animals. For example, they note that the clones' surrogate mothers suffer a higher rate of serious complications or death due to an unusually high percentage of late-term miscarriages and high birth weights of their cloned young. For every successfully cloned animal, dozens—if not hundreds—of cloned embryos die before birth. And the clones are also documented to have more birth defects, to develop more serious illnesses, and to be more likely to die prematurely than animals who are conceived naturally.

In addition, the critics point out that a cloned pet will not be identical in looks or personality to its progenitor. As in the case of CC, it may not have the same coloring as the original pet. And because genetics is not the sole determinant of personality—environment is also a contributor—it will not have the same personality or temperament as its genetic donor. In short, it will be a completely different animal from the original. The owners of the cloned kittens disagree with this assessment, however, and claim that their kittens behave exactly the same as the cats from which they were cloned.

Many of the arguments put forth by supporters and critics of animal cloning are also used in the debate over human cloning. The authors in the following chapter consider these and other perspectives as they examine the ethics of cloning.

*"We believe . . . that attempts to produce a
cloned child would be highly unethical."*

Reproductive Cloning Demeans Human Life

President's Council on Bioethics

In 2001 George W. Bush formed the President's Council on Bioethics to study advances in biotechnology—such as cloning and stem cell research—and advise him on the ethical matters raised by these issues. The following viewpoint is excerpted from the executive summary of the council's report to the president, *Human Cloning and Human Dignity*. The council argues that the rationales offered for using cloning technology to produce children overlook the well-being of the cloned child. Current cloning technology has an extremely high failure rate; there is no way to safely increase the success rate without sacrificing human embryos in the process. In addition, the council argues that cloned children would suffer from identity problems that would compromise their human dignity and individuality. It recommends against cloning to produce children.

As you read, consider the following questions:
1. What purposes might "cloning-to-produce-children" serve, according to the authors?
2. What five concerns does the council have regarding cloning-to-produce-children?

President's Council on Bioethics, *Human Cloning and Human Dignity*. New York: Public Affairs, 2002.

The intense attention given to human cloning in both its potential uses, for reproduction as well as for research, strongly suggests that people do not regard it as just another new technology. Instead, we see it as something quite different, something that touches fundamental aspects of our humanity. The notion of cloning raises issues about identity and individuality, the meaning of having children, the difference between procreation and manufacture, and the relationship between the generations. It also raises new questions about the manipulation of some human beings for the benefit of others, the freedom and value of biomedical inquiry, our obligation to heal the sick (and its limits), and the respect and protection owed to nascent human life.

Finally, the legislative debates over human cloning raise large questions about the relationship between science and society, especially about whether society can or should exercise ethical and prudential control over biomedical technology and the conduct of biomedical research. Rarely has such a seemingly small innovation raised such big questions. . . .

Fair and Accurate Terminology

There is today much confusion about the terms used to discuss human cloning, regarding both the activity involved and the entities that result. The Council stresses the importance of striving not only for accuracy but also for fairness, especially because the choice of terms can decisively affect the way questions are posed, and hence how answers are given. We have sought terminology that most accurately conveys the descriptive reality of the matter, in order that the moral arguments can then proceed on the merits. We have resisted the temptation to solve the moral questions by artful redefinition or by denying to some morally crucial element a name that makes clear that there is a moral question to be faced.

On the basis of (1) a careful analysis of the act of cloning, and its relation to the means by which it is accomplished and the purposes it may serve, and (2) an extensive critical examination of alternative terminologies, the Council has adopted the following definitions for the most important terms in the matter of human cloning:

Cloning: A form of reproduction in which offspring result

not from the chance union of egg and sperm (sexual reproduction) but from the deliberate replication of the genetic makeup of another single individual (asexual reproduction).

Human cloning: The asexual production of a new human organism that is, at all stages of development, genetically virtually identical to a currently existing or previously existing human being. It would be accomplished by introducing the nuclear material of a human somatic cell (donor) into an oocyte (egg) whose own nucleus has been removed or inactivated, yielding a product that has a human genetic constitution virtually identical to the donor of the somatic cell. (This procedure is known as "somatic cell nuclear transfer," or SCNT). We have declined to use the terms "reproductive cloning" and "therapeutic cloning." We have chosen instead to use the following designations:

Cloning-to-produce-children: Production of a cloned human embryo, formed for the (proximate) purpose of initiating a pregnancy, with the (ultimate) goal of producing a child who will be genetically virtually identical to a currently existing or previously existing individual.

Cloning-for-biomedical-research: Production of a cloned human embryo, formed for the (proximate) purpose of using it in research or for extracting its stem cells, with the (ultimate) goals of gaining scientific knowledge of normal and abnormal development and of developing cures for human diseases.

Cloned human embryo: (a) A human embryo resulting from the nuclear transfer process (as contrasted with a human embryo arising from the union of egg and sperm). (b) The immediate (and developing) product of the initial act of cloning, accomplished by successful SCNT, whether used subsequently in attempts to produce children or in biomedical research. . . .

The Ethics of Cloning-to-Produce-Children

Two separate national-level reports on human cloning, concluded that attempts to clone a human being would be unethical at this time due to safety concerns and the likelihood of harm to those involved. The Council concurs in this conclusion. But we have extended the work of these distinguished bodies by undertaking a broad ethical examination of the merits of, and difficulties with, cloning-to-produce-children.

Cloning-to-produce-children might serve several purposes. It might allow infertile couples or others to have genetically related children; permit couples at risk of conceiving a child with a genetic disease to avoid having an afflicted child; allow the bearing of a child who could become an ideal transplant donor for a particular patient in need; enable a parent to keep a living connection with a dead or dying child or spouse; or enable individuals or society to try to "replicate" individuals of great talent or beauty. These purposes have been defended by appeals to the goods of freedom, existence (as opposed to nonexistence), and well-being—all vitally important ideals.

Problems with Human Cloning

There are a host of problems with human cloning that humanity has yet to address. Who are the parents of a clone produced in a laboratory? The donor of the genetic material? The donor of the egg into which the material is transferred? The scientist who manipulates unwanted cells from anonymous donors and facilitates the production of a new life? Who will provide the love and care this embryo, fetus, and then child will need—especially when mistakes are made and it would be easier simply to discard "it." The problems become legion when having children is removed from the context of marriage and even from responsible parenthood.

John F. Kilner, *Dignity*, Spring 2001.

A major weakness in these arguments supporting cloning-to-produce-children is that they overemphasize the freedom, desires, and control of parents, and pay insufficient attention to the well-being of the cloned child-to-be. The Council holds that, once the child-to-be is carefully considered, these arguments are not sufficient to overcome the powerful case against engaging in cloning-to-produce-children.

First, cloning-to-produce-children would violate the principles of the ethics of human research. Given the high rates of morbidity and mortality in the cloning of other mammals, we believe that cloning-to-produce-children would be extremely unsafe, and that attempts to produce a cloned child would be highly unethical. Indeed, our moral analysis of this matter leads us to conclude that this is not, as is sometimes implied, a merely temporary objection, easily removed by the improvement of technique. We offer reasons for believing that the safety risks might be enduring, and offer arguments in support of a strong conclusion: that conducting experiments in an effort to make cloning-to-produce-children less dangerous would itself be an unacceptable violation of the norms of research ethics. *There seems to be no ethical way to try to discover whether cloning-to-produce-children can become safe, now or in the future.*

Categories of Concern

If carefully considered, the concerns about safety also begin to reveal the ethical principles that should guide a broader assessment of cloning-to-produce-children: the principles of freedom, equality, and human dignity. To appreciate the broader human significance of cloning-to-produce-children, one needs first to reflect on the meaning of having children; the meaning of asexual, as opposed to sexual, reproduction; the importance of origins and genetic endowment for identity and sense of self; the meaning of exercising greater human control over the processes and "products" of human reproduction; and the difference between begetting and making. Reflecting on these topics, the Council has identified five categories of concern regarding cloning-to-produce-children. (Different Council Members give varying moral weight to these different concerns.)

Problems of identity and individuality. Cloned children may experience serious problems of identity both because each will be genetically virtually identical to a human being who has already lived and because the expectations for their lives may be shadowed by constant comparisons to the life of the "original."

Concerns regarding manufacture. Cloned children would be the first human beings whose entire genetic makeup is selected in advance. They might come to be considered more like products of a designed manufacturing process than "gifts" whom their parents are prepared to accept as they are. Such an attitude toward children could also contribute to increased commercialization and industrialization of human procreation.

The Effects on Society and Family

The prospect of a new eugenics. Cloning, if successful, might serve the ends of privately pursued eugenic enhancement, either by avoiding the genetic defects that may arise when human reproduction is left to chance, or by preserving and perpetuating outstanding genetic traits, including the possibility, someday in the future, of using cloning to perpetuate genetically engineered enhancements.

Troubled family relations. By confounding and transgressing the natural boundaries between generations, cloning could strain the social ties between them. Fathers could become "twin brothers" to their "sons"; mothers could give birth to their genetic twins; and grandparents would also be the "genetic parents" of their grandchildren. Genetic relation to only one parent might produce special difficulties for family life.

Effects on society. Cloning-to-produce-children would affect not only the direct participants but also the entire society that allows or supports this activity. Even if practiced on a small scale, it could affect the way society looks at children and set a precedent for future nontherapeutic interventions into the human genetic endowment or novel forms of control by one generation over the next. In the absence of wisdom regarding these matters, prudence dictates caution and restraint.

Conclusion: For some or all of these reasons, the Council is in full agreement that cloning-to-produce-children is not only unsafe but also morally unacceptable, and ought not to be attempted.

"If we shouldn't call a person created by cloning a 'clone,' what should we call him? Answer: a person."

Reproductive Cloning Does Not Demean Human Life

Gregory E. Pence

In the following viewpoint, Gregory E. Pence exposes what he says are ten myths about human cloning. He contends that clones, like the test-tube babies that came before them, would be especially loved and wanted by their parents because of the difficulty and cost of their conception. He also questions how a new way of making a family could possibly be wrong. Furthermore, Pence doubts that clones would be psychologically or physically harmed by being born a clone since children's origins do not affect the rights they have as persons once they are born. Pence is a bioethicist who lectures on philosophy and medical ethics at the University of Alabama.

As you read, consider the following questions:

1. According to Pence, why is a clone not an exact duplicate of the original ancestor?
2. How does the author refute the claim that cloning reduces biological diversity?
3. What is Pence's argument against the claim that only selfish people would clone a child?

The top ten myths about human cloning:
   1. Cloning Xeroxes a person.

Cloning merely re-creates the genes of the ancestor, not what he has learned or experienced. Technically, it re-creates the genotype, not the phenotype. (Even at that, only 99% of those genes get re-created because 1% of such a child's genes would come from those in the egg—mitochondrial DNA). Conventional wisdom holds that about half of who we are comes from our genes, the other half, from the environment. Cloning cannot re-create what in us came from the environment; it also cannot re-create memories.

The false belief that cloning re-creates a person stems in part from the common, current false belief in simplistic, genetic reductionism, i.e., that a person really is just determined by his genes. No reputable geneticist or psychologist believes this.

Children Would Be Loved

2. Human cloning is replication or making children into commodities.

Opponents of cloning often use these words to beg the question, to assume that children created by parents by a new method would not be loved. Similar things were said about "test tube" babies, who turned out to be some of the most-wanted, most-loved babies ever created in human history.

Indeed, the opposite is true: evolution has created us with sex drives such that, if we do not carefully use contraception, children occur. Because children get created this way without being wanted, sexual reproduction is more likely to create unwanted, and hence possibly unloved, children than human cloning.

Lawyers opposing cloning have a special reason for using these pejorative words. If cloning is just a new form of human reproduction, then it is Constitutionally protected from interference by the state. Several Supreme Court decisions declare that all forms of human reproduction, including the right not to reproduce, cannot be abridged by government.

Use of words such as "replication" and "commodification" also assumes artificial wombs or commercial motives; about these fallacies, see below.

Neither Uniformity Nor Diversity

3. Human cloning reduces biological diversity.

Population genetics says otherwise. Six billion people now exist, soon to be eight billion, and most of them reproduce. Cloning requires in vitro fertilization, which is expensive and inefficient, with only a 20% success rate. Since 1978, at most a half million babies have been produced this way, or at most, one out of 12,000 babies.

Over decades and with such great numbers, populations follow the Law of Regression to the Mean. This means that, even if someone tried to create a superior race by cloning, it would fail, because cloned people would have children with non-cloned people, and resulting genetic hybrids would soon be normalized.

Cloning is simply a tool. It could be used with the motive of creating uniformity (but would fail, because of above), or it [could] be used for the opposite reason, to try to increase diversity (which would also fail, for the same reason).

A Clone Is a Real Person

4. People created by cloning would be less ensouled than normal humans, or would be sub-human.

A human who had the same number of chromosomes as a child created sexually, who was gestated by a woman, and who talked, felt, and spoke as any other human, would ethically be human and a person. It is by now a principle of ethics that the origins of a person, be it from mixed-race parents, unmarried parents, in vitro fertilization, or a gay male couple hiring a surrogate mother, do not affect the personhood of the child born. The same would be true of a child created by cloning (who, of course, has to be gestated for nine months by a woman).

Every deviation from normal reproduction has always been faced with this fear. Children created by sperm donation, in vitro fertilization, and surrogate motherhood were predicted to be less-than-human, but were not.

A variation predicts that while, in fact, they will not be less-than-human, people will treat them this way and hence, such children will [be] harmed. This objection reifies prejudice and makes it an ethical justification, which it is wrong to do. The correct response to prejudice is to expose it for what it is, combat it with reason and with evidence, not validate it as an ethical reason.

A Clone Has Rights

5. People created by cloning could be used for spare organs for normal humans.

Nothing could be done to a person created by cloning that right now could not be done to your brother or to a person's twin. The U. S. Constitution strongly implies that once a human fetus is outside the womb and alive, he has rights. Decisions backing this up give him rights to inherit property, rights not to suffer discrimination because of disability, and rights to U.S. citizenship.

A variation of this myth assumes that a dictator could make cloned humans into special SWAT teams or suicidal bombers. But nothing about originating people this way gives anyone any special power over the resulting humans, who would have free will. Besides, if a dictator wants to create such assassins, he need not wait for cloning but can take orphans and try to indoctrinate them now in isolated camps.

Pure Science Fiction

6. All people created from the same genotype would be raised in batches and share secret empathy or communication.

Pure science fiction. If I wanted to recreate the genotype of my funny Uncle Harry, why would my wife want to gestate 5 or 6 other babies at the same time? Indeed, we now know that the womb cannot support more than 2-3 fetuses without creating a likely disability in one. Guidelines now call for no more than two embryos to be introduced by in vitro fertilization, which of course is required to use cloning.

Such assumptions about cloned humans being created in batches are linked to nightmarish science fiction scenarios where human society has been destroyed and where industrialized machines have taken over human reproduction. But this is just someone's nightmare, not facts upon which to base state and federal laws.

7. Scientists who work on human cloning are evil or motivated by bad motives.

Clones and Identical Twins

Some have objected that cloning threatens their sense of identity, and assert that they find it easier to get out of bed in the morning knowing that they are unique. Others assert that cloning, by making it possible to duplicate people, will cheapen individual lives.

Both make false assumptions about what is possible through cloning. Those who find it easier to get out of bed knowing they are unique must be grateful that they do not have an identical twin. For identical twins have much . . . in common. . . . Identical twins are usually raised in the same household by the same parents, in the same culture, facing the same trends and pressures at the same times in their lives.

And yet identical twins tend to express no misgivings about living in a world which also contains a clone.

Alonzo Fyfe, www.reproductivecloning.net, 2001.

The stuff of Hollywood and scary writers. Scientists are just people. Most of them have kids of their own and care a lot for kids. No one wants to bring a handicapped child into the world. Movies and novels never portray life scientists with sympathy. This anti-science prejudice started with Mary Shelley's *Frankenstein* and continues with nefarious scientists working for the Government on *The X Files*. People who call themselves scientists and grandstand for television, such as Richard Seed and Brigette Boisselier of the Raelians,[1] are not real scientists but people who use the aura of science to gain attention. Real scientists don't spend all their time flying around the world to be on TV but stay at home in their clinics, doing their work.

No Artificial Wombs

8. Babies created by cloning could be grown in artificial wombs.

Nope, sorry. Medicine has been trying for fifty years to create an artificial womb, but has never come close to succeeding. Indeed, controversial experiments in 1973 on liveborn fetuses in studying artificial wombs effectively shut down such research. Finally, if anything like such wombs existed, we could save premature babies who haven't developed

1. The Raelians are a cult that claimed to have cloned a child in February 2004.

lung function, but unfortunately, we still can't—premature babies who can't breathe at all die.

Thus, any human baby still needs a human woman to gestate him for at least six months, and to be healthy, nine months. This puts the lie to many science fiction stories and to many predictions about cloning and industrial reproduction.

What Is a Good Reason to Have a Child?

9. Only selfish people want to create a child by cloning.

First, this assumes that ordinary people don't create children for selfish reasons, such as a desire to have someone take care of them in old age, a desire to see part of themselves continue after death, and/or the desire to leave their estate to someone. Many people are hypocritical or deceived about why they came to have children. Very few people just decide that they want to bring more joy into the world, and hence create a child to raise and support for life as an end-in-himself. Let's be honest here.

Second, a couple using cloning need not create a copy of one of them. As said above, Uncle Harry could be a prime candidate. On the other hand, if a couple chooses a famous person, critics accuse them of creating designer babies. Either way, they can't win: if they re-create one of their genotypes, they are narcissistic; if they choose someone else's genes, they're guilty of creating designer babies.

In general, why should a couple using cloning have a higher justification required of them than a couple using sexual reproduction? If we ask: what counts as a good reason for creating a child, then why should cloning have any special test that is not required for sexual reproduction? Indeed, and more generally, what right does government have to require, or judge, any couple's reasons for having a child, even if they are seen by others to be selfish? Couples desiring to use cloning should not bear an undue burden of justification.

Just a Tool

10. Human cloning is inherently evil: it can only be used for bad purposes by bad people.

No, it's just a tool, just another way to create a family. A long legacy in science fiction novels and movies make the word "cloning" so fraught with bad connotations that it can hardly be used in any discussion that purports to be impartial. It is like discussing equal rights for women by starting to discuss whether "the chicks" would fare better with equal rights. To most people, "cloning" implies selfish parents, crazy scientists, and out-of-control technology, so a fair discussion using this word isn't possible. Perhaps the phrase, "somatic cell nuclear transplantation" is better, even if it's a scientific mouthful.

So if we shouldn't call a person created by cloning, a "clone," what should we call him? Answer: a person.

> *"Cloning might be the perfect sin. It just might break all Ten Commandments at once."*

Therapeutic Cloning Is Immoral

Terrence Jeffrey

In 2004 researchers in South Korea created a new "line" of stem cells from cloned human embryos to use in stem cell research. In the following viewpoint, Terrence Jeffrey argues that of the 242 eggs that were produced, 30 eggs developed into cloned embryos, and of these, only one cloned embryo resulted in a new stem cell line. Jeffrey argues that this research resulted in the massive loss of human life and in the process broke all of the Ten Commandments. In order for the research to be moral, he concludes, it must not harm any humans. Therefore, therapeutic cloning is immoral. Jeffrey is a syndicated columnist.

As you read, consider the following questions:
1. What is SCNT-hES-1, according to Jeffrey?
2. What is a SCID mouse, according to the author?
3. How does therapeutic cloning break the commandment "Thou shalt not bear false witness against thy neighbor," in Jeffrey's opinion?

Terrence Jeffrey, "Does Cloning Break All Ten Commandments?" www.townhall. com, February 18, 2004. Copyright © 2003 by Creators Syndicate. Reproduced by permission.

There are those who argue that "therapeutic" cloning—in which a human embryo is cloned and killed—is a great advancement for the human race. But when I read the recent *Science* article describing how researchers in South Korea had cloned human embryos, it occurred to me that cloning might be the perfect sin. It just might break all Ten Commandments at once.

Follow my thinking on this.

Creating a New Line of Stem Cells

In Korea, 16 women volunteered for "ovarian stimulation." That yielded 242 human eggs. Researchers managed to "squeeze" the nucleus from 176 of these and replace it with the nucleus of another cell from the same donor. These were chemically treated to induce division. In 30, a cloned embryo—a little girl identical to her mother—began to develop.

In the womb, these girls could grow into babies. But the researchers did not create them to live; they created them to die. (In *Science*, they mention that "overwhelming ethical constraints preclude any reproductive cloning attempts.")

Why did they kill these embryonic girls? To develop a line of cells they call "SCNT-hES-1." That stands for: Somatic cell nuclear transfer-human embryonic stem cells-1.

In the quest for SCNT-hES-1, they dismembered the embryos, trying to isolate their stem cells. In 20, they succeeded. In just one, they managed to culture the stem cells, creating a "line."

Thirty died in embryo so SCNT-hES-1 could live—in the testicles of a mutant mouse, called a SCID, which lacks an immune system and thus won't reject human tissue.

This isn't science fiction; it's in *Science*.

"When undifferentiated SCNT-hES-1 were injected into the testis of SCID mice," explained the researchers, the cells grew into tumors that included "differentiated" human muscle, bone and other tissue.

Refine this process, and you can, as the researchers put it, "generate potentially unlimited sources of undifferentiated cells for research, with potential applications in tissue repair and transplantation medicine."

An ailing body could be patched back together with pieces

torn from its own clone. Dr. Frankenstein's monster lives—
and soon will strain at its straps.

The Ten Commandments

So, how does this square with the Ten Commandments?
Take them in order:

1. Thou shalt not have strange gods before Me.

Is there a stranger god than a scientist who usurps the
Creator by giving and taking life in a laboratory?

Thornhill. © 1998 by the *North County Times*. Reproduced by permission.

2. Thou shalt not take the name of the Lord thy God in
vain.

(As a Catholic, I'll rely on the analysis of the Catholic Catechism for this one.) "God calls each one by name," says the
catechism. "Everyone's name is sacred. . . . It bears respect as
a sign of the dignity of the one who bears it."

Cloning strips dignity from embryos by creating and killing
them without naming them, or even properly calling them
human beings. They're not Sarah or Stephen; they're steps on
the way to SCNT-hES.

3. Remember that thou keep holy the Sabbath day.

Cloning's abuse of life goes around the clock. They don't empty the petri dishes Saturday and start again Monday.

4. Honor thy father and mother.

Cloning disrupts the unbroken chain of mother-father procreation that has perpetuated the race since Creation. Egg donors aren't honored as mothers; fatherhood is nullified.

5. Thou shalt not kill.

"Therapeutic" cloning creates embryos to kill them. Reproductive cloning can only be achieved if many embryos are sacrificed to perfect the process.

6. Thou shalt not commit adultery.

Cloning uses women to create children by means other than their husbands.

7. Thou shalt not steal.

"Therapeutic" cloning steals stem cells from embryos; all cloning steals a child's right to a natural father, conception, gestation and a unique place in the human family.

8. Thou shalt not bear false witness against thy neighbor.

Cloning is predicated on the lie that a human embryo is not a human life.

9. Thou shalt not covet thy neighbor's wife.

Because of the many human eggs cloning demands, practitioners will covet women as donors.

10. Thou shalt not covet thy neighbor's house, nor his field, nor his servant, nor his handmaid, nor his ox, nor his ass, nor anything that is his.

Therapeutic cloners covet an embryo's stem cells. And is it unreasonable to assume the drive to clone arises from an inordinate desire for money or power?

Cloning Is Immoral

I'm neither a scientist nor a theologian, and perhaps my analysis of the Ten Commandments here is imperfect. But for cloning to be moral it must comply with all 10, and for it to merit legality—even in a secular society—it cannot violate any precept necessary to protect our neighbors from harm. Let's see its defenders explain how that could be.

"Cloning does represent 'the desire to exert our will over every aspect of our surroundings.' But such a desire is not immoral—it is a mark of virtue."

Therapeutic Cloning Is Moral

Alex Epstein

South Korean scientists who created a new line of stem cells from cloned human embryos have made a huge medical breakthrough in the possible treatment of many diseases, argues Alex Epstein in the following viewpoint. This technology is pro-life, he contends, since it will be used to save human lives. He rejects the claim that stem cell research is immoral because it amounts to "playing God." In fact, he insists, it would be immoral not to use whatever technology is available—including cloning—to improve life for human beings. Epstein is a writer for the Ayn Rand Institute, a public policy research organization.

As you read, consider the following questions:
1. How does the author describe cloned human embryos?
2. How does Epstein respond to opponents' arguments that cloning is "playing God"?
3. What legitimate uses would reproductive cloning have, in Epstein's opinion?

In a huge breakthrough for medical progress, scientists from South Korea have finally created a cloned human embryo and extracted its stem cells—a feat that makes life-saving embryonic stem-cell treatments that much closer to reality. Instead of taking this thrilling news as an opportunity to celebrate cloning, politicians and intellectuals are once again calling for bans. Some seek to ban all cloning, while others oppose "only" reproductive cloning. Although each group claims the moral high ground, both positions are profoundly immoral. Any attempt to ban human cloning technology should be rejected permanently, because cloning—therapeutic and reproductive—is morally good.

Consider first therapeutic cloning, which opponents perversely condemn as "antilife." Senator Sam Brownback, who has sponsored a Congressional ban on all cloning, says therapeutic cloning is "creating human life to destroy [it]." President [George W.] Bush calls it "growing human beings for spare body parts."

Cloning Is Pro-Life

In fact, therapeutic cloning is a highly pro-life technology, since cloned embryos can be used to extract medically potent embryonic stem cells. A cloned embryo is created by inserting the nucleus of a human body cell into a denucleated egg, which is then induced to divide until it reaches the embryo stage. These embryos are not human beings, but microscopic bits of protoplasm the width of a human hair. They have the potential to grow into human beings, but actual human beings are the ones dying for lack of this technology. The embryonic stem cells extracted from a cloned embryo can become any other type of human cell. In the future, they may be used to develop pancreatic cells for curing diabetes, cardiac muscle cells for curing heart disease, brain cells for curing Alzheimer's—or even entire new organs for transplantation. "There's not an area of medicine that this technology will not potentially impact," says Nobel laureate Harold Varmus.

Opponents of therapeutic cloning know all this, but are unmoved. This is because their fundamental objection is not that therapeutic cloning is antilife, but that it entails "playing God"—i.e., remaking nature to serve human purposes. "[Hu-

Saving and Healing Lives

When human life begins . . . is a profoundly religious question in a profoundly religious country, profoundly dedicated to the proposition that our freedom to faithfully interpret our faith is the core of American life. For nearly all Jews, most Muslims, many Buddhists, and many Protestants, it is not only permissible to use human blastocysts to create stem cell lines, it is morally imperative—it must be done if it can lead to saving lives or healing. As an orthodox Jew, I understand the blastocyst, made in the lab, at the very first stages of division, prior to the time it could even successfully be transferred to a woman's body at just what it is at that moment: a cluster of primitive cells. It does not have the moral status of a human child—it lacks a mother's womb, its existence is only theoretical without this, and even in the course of a normal pregnancy a blastocyst at 3 days is far before our tradition considers it a human person. While I respect that this is a difference in theology, and while I understand the passion and the conviction of those for whom the blastocyst is a person from the moment of fertilization, I do not believe this, and it is matter of faith for me as well. My passion and my conviction are toward the suffering of the one I see in need, ill, or wounded—for Jews and Muslims, the commandment to attend to this suffering is core to our faiths. Jewish organizations from Hadassah to the rabbinic and lay boards of all national Jewish denominations speak in one voice on this matter: human embryonic stem cell research is an activity of *pekuah nefesh*, saving and healing broken lives, and of *tikkun olam*—repairing an unfinished natural world.

Laurie Zoloth, testimony before U.S. Senate Committee on Commerce, Science, and Transportation, September 29, 2004.

man cloning] would be taking a major step into making man himself simply another one of the man-made things," says Leon Kass, chairman of the President's Council on Bioethics. "Human nature becomes merely the last part of nature to succumb to the technological project, which turns all of nature into raw material at human disposal." Columnist Armstrong Williams condemns all cloning as "human egotism, or the desire to exert our will over every aspect of our surroundings," and cautions: "We're not God."

A Mark of Virtue

The one truth in the anticloning position is that cloning does represent "the desire to exert our will over every aspect of our surroundings." But such a desire is not immoral—it is a mark of virtue. Using technology to alter nature is a requirement of human life. It is what brought man from the cave to civilization. Where would we be without the men who "exerted their will" over their surroundings and constructed the first hut, cottage, and skyscraper? Every advance in human history is part of "the technological project," and has made man's life longer, healthier, and happier. These advances are produced by those who hold the premise that suffering and disease are a curse, not to be humbly accepted as "God's will," but to be fought proudly with all the power of man's rational mind.

The same virtue applies to reproductive cloning—which, despite the ridiculous, horror-movie scenarios conjured up by its opponents, would simply result in time-separated twins just as human as anyone else. Once it becomes safe, reproductive cloning will have legitimate uses for infertile couples and for preventing the transmission of genetic diseases. Even more important, it is significant as an early form of a tremendous value: genetic engineering, which most anticloners object to because as such it entails "playing God" with the genetic makeup of one's child. At stake with reproductive cloning is not only whether you can conceive a child who shares your genetic makeup, but whether you have the right to improve the genetic makeup of your children: to prevent them from getting genetic diseases, to prolong their lifespan or to improve their physical appearance. You should have such rights just as you have the right to vaccinate your children or to fit them with braces.

The mentalities that denounce cloning and "playing God" have consistently opposed technological progress, especially in medicine. They objected to anesthesia, smallpox inoculations, contraception, heart transplants, in vitro fertilization—on the grounds that these innovations were "unnatural" and contrary to God's will. To let them cripple biotechnological progress by banning cloning would be a moral abomination.

"Many of the ethical concerns raised by human cloning apply to this reckless disregard for the integrity of animal life."

Animal Cloning Is Unethical

Wayne Pacelle

Cloning animals—for pets or for agriculture or research—is completely superfluous and fraught with hazards, argues Wayne Pacelle in the following viewpoint. He maintains that too many animals are in shelters waiting to be adopted to spend money to clone a pet. In addition, due to the many risks it poses, cloning animals amounts to a form of animal cruelty. Pacelle is the president and CEO of the Humane Society of the United States.

As you read, consider the following questions:

1. What makes a cloned animal different from its forebear, according to Pacelle?
2. Why would production of genetically identical farm animals pose a threat to food security, in the author's opinion?
3. What are some of the problems experienced by the "success stories" of cloned farm animals, according to the author?

With the arrival of Little Nicky, a kitten cloned to duplicate a Dallas woman's deceased pet, animal cloning has moved from closed-door laboratories to commercial application. The $50,000 feline was delivered by Genetic Savings & Clone, the playfully named company catering to particularly devoted pet owners.

While the intentions of the pet owners are understandable, the practice itself is rife with hazard and requires a decisive response from policy-makers. There are many practical problems with pet cloning, not the least of which is that the genetic duplicate may turn out to act, and even look, different from its forebear. Each creature—shaped in part by life experience—is more than an embodiment of his or her DNA. A cloned animal may look much the same and bring back happy memories for pet lovers, but the creature they are looking at is not the same animal.

Not Worth It

More to the point, with millions of healthy and adoptable cats and dogs being killed each year for lack of suitable homes, it's a little frivolous to be cloning departed pets. The challenge is not to find new, absurdly expensive ways to create animals, but to curb the growth of pet populations and to foster an ethic in society that prompts people to adopt and shelter creatures in need of loving homes.

Pet cloning is simply not worth repeating. Behind this one little kitten are far grander schemes to clone animals for use in agriculture and research. Before such projects become the norm, we should pause and think carefully about where it is leading—for animals and for humanity.

It was big news some years ago when scientists in Scotland announced the cloning of Dolly the sheep. This new technology marked a decisive moment in our ability to manipulate the natural world to suit our designs. Dolly has long since passed, afflicted by a lung disease that typically occurs in much older sheep. Since her dramatic birth—and her pitiful decline—scientists have turned out clones for mice, rabbits, goats, pigs, cows and now cats. Cloned horses and dogs, we are promised, are on the way. But behind every heralded success are hundreds of monstrous failures.

Sutton. © 2002 by the *Village Voice*. Reproduced by permission.

Cloning and Agribusiness

As all of this has unfolded, policy-makers have stood idly by, failing to place any restraints of law and ethics on corporations and scientists who are tinkering here with the most fundamental elements of biology. We hear indignation and expressions of well-founded concern about human cloning. But we hear hardly a word of doubt or moral concern about the idea of animal cloning, much less about the particular animals subjected to these experiments. It won't be long before biotech companies in the hire of agribusiness announce plans to sell commercial clones as food. Cloned ham, steak, and even drumsticks may be served at retail operations in the future, and there's no law to forbid the sale of meat or milk from clones produced in a laboratory.

Like pet cloning, the cloning of farm animals is monumentally unnecessary. Farmers are already producing so much meat that they must find export markets to turn a profit. As for milk, it's cheaper than bottled water. The dairy industry recently "culled" tens of thousands of healthy dairy cows in order to depress production.

Small farmers, already put at a disadvantage by mounting debt and mechanized competitors, will be further marginalized as cloning practices become commonplace. More than ever, they'll be at the mercy of corporate factory farms to purchase their supply of clones.

Consumers face threats of a different sort. Who knows if consuming meat and milk from clones is safe? A recent Food and Drug Administration symposium addressed this issue, but the confident declarations that the animal products are safe didn't seem all that reassuring: Just one misstep could be catastrophic. With mad cow, foot-and-mouth, avian flu and other diseases now posing a greater threat in our globalized agricultural markets, the production of genetically identical animals would pose serious threats to food security. Genetic variation, already low from conventional breeding, would also be almost eliminated by cloning.

Grievous Problems

As for the animals in our factory farms, cloning is the final assault on their well-being and dignity. When the FDA held a public consultation on animal cloning in November 2003, researchers reported a graphic list of problems for clones and their surrogate mothers in cattle, pigs, sheep and goats—a string of developmental abnormalities and a host of deaths before, during and after birth. The animals being cloned exhibit grievous problems, such as cows with grossly enlarged udders, major leg problems and other forms of lameness. And these are the very animals trumpeted as success stories.

Of the largest group of clones yet—produced by Cyagra, which clones cattle—few embryos survived to term, and of those that did, a third then died by the age of 1 year. The FDA's report, "Animal Cloning: A Risk Assessment" put a nice spin on this when it said that "the proportion of live, normal births appears to be increasing." In other words, the situation has improved from atrocious to very bad.

It is time for Congress and the FDA and other regulatory

bodies to engage in the animal-cloning debate. Many of the ethical concerns raised by human cloning apply to this reckless disregard for the integrity of animal life. Should such questions be left entirely to scientists and corporations, since they have an intellectual and commercial stake in these projects? Our government alone can stand up for the public interest in preventing this cruelty.

Cloning is a startling procedure, to be sure, and many scientists would have us view it as some inevitable stage in our technological development. But humanity's progress is not always defined by scientific innovation alone. Cloning—both human and animal—is one of those cases in which progress is defined by the exercise of wisdom and of self-restraint.

*"The advantages that may accrue from
producing genetically identical laboratory
animal strains without inbreeding could
. . . prove very helpful."*

Animal Cloning Could Be Beneficial

Ian Wilmut and Keith Campbell

Ian Wilmut, an embryologist, led the team of scientists at the
Roslin Institute in Edinburgh, Scotland, that produced the
cloned sheep Dolly. Keith Campbell is a cell biologist and
embryologist who worked with Wilmut to clone Dolly. The
following viewpoint is an excerpt from their book *The Second
Creation: Dolly and the Age of Biological Control.* They assert
that cloning animals has many useful applications for science.
For example, cloning can produce genetically similar laboratory animals while avoiding many of the problems associated
with inbreeding. In addition, cloning can be used to improve
dairy herds more quickly than conventional means, and it
could possibly help endangered animals reproduce.

As you read, consider the following questions:
1. According to the authors, how does too much
   homozygosity adversely affect laboratory animals?
2. How many years would it take a farmer to improve his
   dairy herd using artificial insemination as opposed to
   cloning, according to Wilmut and Campbell?
3. How do the authors refute the argument that cloning
   would not increase diversity among breeding
   populations?

With cloning firmly established in the modern canon, it is as if the science and techniques of biology have been liberated from constraints that once seemed inviolable. We and our descendants must wait and see what the world makes of this liberation, or rather, we must try to see that the new power is put only to good and proper use. It would be foolish to underestimate the potential. Tomorrow's biology, swollen with the new techniques and insights that will accrue from the science and technologies of cloning, now promises us a measure of control over life's processes that in practice will seem absolute. It would be dangerous ever to suppose that we can understand all of life's processes exhaustively: this would lead us into the Greek sin of hubris, with all the penalties that follow. Yet our descendants will find themselves with power that seems limited only by their imagination—that, plus the laws of physics and the rules of logic.

Prediction is a dangerous game, but it is one we should never stop trying to play. So let us look at what seems feasible in the light of current knowledge. The first and most obvious possibility is to increase the range of species that can be cloned. . . .

Cloning for the Laboratory

Cloning laboratory animals may seem too obvious to be worth comment, but there is more to it than meets the eye. The central aim, of course, is to produce animals for experimentation that are genetically uniform, so that when scientists try out a particular drug or training method or other procedure, they know that any differences they perceive are due to the procedure and not to genetic differences between the animals. But there are various difficulties. Notably, the traditional way—and up to now the only way—to produce genetically uniform strains of, say, mice has been by inbreeding. Closely related individuals are mated, and their offspring are remated, until a population is produced that is all of a muchness.

But as everyone knows, such inbreeding is dangerous. It is for this reason that various genetic disorders, including porphyria and hemophilia, have bedeviled various royal houses in Europe. The problem lies with excess *homozygosity*. Every individual inherits one set of genes from one parent, and another set from the other parent. If the two parents are not closely related, then the two sets of genes will differ somewhat. You might, for example, inherit a gene for red hair from your mother, and a gene for dark hair from your father. Then you are said to be *heterozygous* for that particular gene for hair color. But if you inherited a gene for red hair from both parents, you would be homozygous for that hair color gene. The trouble begins when one of the genes in a matching pair is a deleterious mutant—for example, the one that produces cystic fibrosis. If you inherit a cystic fibrosis mutant from one parent and a normal gene from the other, then you will not suffer from the disease; your heterozygosity saves you. But if you inherit the CF gene from both parents, you will be affected. Of course, only a minority of genes are as harmful as the CF mutant, but the principle applies broadly, and too much homozygosity leads to the general loss of fitness known as inbreeding depression.

Uniform and Heterozygous

So if you produce laboratory animals simply by inbreeding, then you will perforce produce a great deal of homozygosity, which is likely to lead to inbreeding depression. In fact *most* attempts to produce purebred strains of laboratory mice have failed. The strains that exist today are the minority that have survived inbreeding, fortunate beasts that happen, by chance, to lack a significant number of genes that are deleterious so that they avoid the kinds of effects we see in cystic fibrosis. We have to conclude, though, that laboratory mice are genetically peculiar because most animals simply cannot withstand such a high degree of homozygosity. Yet it happens, too, that inbreeding does not produce quite such uniformity as might be supposed. Sometimes there has proved to be a remarkable amount of genetic variation (implying heterozygosity) in laboratory strains that are supposed to be completely uniform.

On the other hand, it would sometimes be good to work with creatures that are more "natural": that is, are more heterozygous. Cloning helps here, as well. It not only offers a route to complete genetic uniformity—at least of the nuclear genes—but also makes it possible to produce strains that are uniform but *not* homozygous. In fact, a highly heterozygous wild mouse—or in principle a wild anything—could be cloned to produce as many genetic facsimiles as required. We are so used to thinking that genetic uniformity can be produced only by inbreeding that we tend to assume that uniformity must imply homozygosity. But consider, say, any one variety of domestic potato. Any particular King Edward or Maris Piper might well be highly heterozygous, but since it is multiplied by cloning (via tubers), each individual potato is genetically similar to all the others, and so the variety as a whole is uniform.

The advantages that may accrue from producing genetically identical laboratory animal strains *without* inbreeding could, as the decades pass, prove very helpful.

Replicating the Elite

Similar considerations—and more—apply to the cloning of farm livestock. On the one hand, farmers seek uniformity: they want to know how their animals are liable to perform under particular conditions, when they are liable to mature, and so on; and so, of course, do their markets. On the other hand, farmers also seek optimum performance, where "optimum" does not necessarily mean "maximum," although increasingly this is the case. Among, say, dairy cattle there is a huge difference between the yield of the milkiest cows, commonly called elite animals, and of the least endowed. A wild cow produces around 300 gallons of milk in a year to feed her solitary calf, while many modern Friesians produce 2,000 gallons and more. Of course, a modern farmer would have a herd of purebred Friesians, but even in one elite herd, there is commonly a twofold difference between the milkiest animals (2,000 gallons) and the average (around 1,000 gallons). In general, farmers seek to bring the average up to the level of the best. But such "improvements" (this is the technical term) take a very long time. The farmer normally improves his herd by impregnating his better cows by AI [artificial insemination] with semen from an elite bull. But only half the calves produced will be female, and each of them takes three years from conception to first lactation (a working year for her own gestation, then a year to mature, then another nine months to produce a calf as a prelude to lactation). In short, raising the standard of a herd even when the farmer has access to the world's best bulls is a slow business. In breeding time, the average animals are commonly considered to be ten years behind the elite.

Ensuring the Safety of Food from Cloned Animals

The FDA commissioned the National Academy of Sciences (NAS) to identify and prioritize any safety concerns that bioengineered and cloned animals might present to food, animals and the environment.

After consulting with pioneers in the field of cloning and holding a public workshop, the NAS published its report, *Animal Biotechnology: Science-Based Concerns*, in August 2002. According to the report, "There is no current evidence that food products derived from adult somatic cell clones or their progeny present a food safety concern." The report recommends collecting additional information about food composition to confirm that these food products are, in fact, safe. Food should be analyzed for such essential ingredients as amino acids, vitamins and minerals and to make sure cloned animal products don't differ from those of normal animals in ways that might affect human health.

Linda Bren, "Cloning: Revolution or Evolution in Animal Production?" *FDA Consumer*, May/June 2003.

There are further complications. Just as animals (and plants) suffer from inbreeding depression when they are too homozygous, they can also experience what [naturalist] Charles Darwin called hybrid vigor when they are outbred and thus highly heterozygous. Farmers of animals, like growers of potatoes, would in general like to combine overall uniformity with individual heterozygosity. In addition, farmers often seek to combine the qualities of different breeds, so that dairy farmers commonly cross Friesian dairy cows with beefy bulls (such as Herefords or Charolais) to produce calves that are good for beef (since only a minority of calves born in a dairy herd are needed as herd replacements). Among sheep farmers, juggling the options between uplands and lowlands, the crossing permutations can be quite bewildering.

Speeding Up the Process

In all such instances where the need is to raise herd quality quickly, and/or to combine uniformity with heterozygosity, cloning has an obvious role. A dairy farmer might improve his herd significantly in ten years by purchasing sperm from an elite bull, but he might achieve the same improvement in one season by furnishing his cows with ready-made embryos that have been cloned from some elite animal. No wonder the Americans invested so much in this technology in the 1980s. Of course, ultrahigh performance does raise special issues of animal welfare—which alone must set limits on what can be done. On the other hand, cloning and embryo transfer could be of particular value in the Third World, where cattle are vital to the economy, where they are often multipurpose (cows might be required to pull carts as well as to provide calves and milk, though they may feed mainly on straw and must withstand tropical heat), and where breeding is particularly difficult because of the many contrasting qualities that are required in any one animal. Whether the economic "incentives" exist to take the new technologies into poor countries is another question.

Cloning for Conservation

Cloning could also be of immense, perhaps even critical, value in animal conservation. Many have doubted this. The critics point out, for example, that the task for conservationists is to maintain the maximum possible genetic diversity within each breeding population and point out, rightly, that cloning does not increase diversity. It merely replicates what is there already. This is precisely the point. Conservationists cannot *add* to the range of genes that currently exists. But they must strive to minimize the rate at which genetic diversity is lost. The great enemy is "genetic drift," the steady loss of genetic variation, generation by generation. When animals breed, each parent passes on only *half* of his or her genes to each offspring. If the animal has hundreds or millions of offspring, like a fly or a codfish, then there is a very good chance that each parent will indeed pass on all of its genes, which will be spread randomly among the many offspring. But an animal like a rhinoceros or an orangutan may have only about half a dozen offspring in a lifetime, so some of its genes are liable to remain uninherited. If the population of rhinos or orangs is large, then any one variant of any one gene is liable to be contained within many different individuals, so the breeding animals should pass on all the genes in the total gene pool. But if the breeding population is low—as it is bound to be if the animal is already rare—then the less common genes may well be contained within only one or a few individuals, and the individual containing the rarest genes may well finish its reproductive life without passing them on. Hence generational loss of variation.

Conservation biologists attempt to minimize loss by genetic drift by complicated breeding schemes intended to ensure that each individual that can breed does indeed mate (while avoiding inbreeding), but these schemes are expensive and difficult to organize. Yet it would be technically easy to take tissue samples (biopsies) from representative members of all the endangered species of mammals that now exist (about 200 at least are priorities), culture them, and then put the cultures in deep freeze. (If the biopsies were simply frozen without culturing them first, they would probably be damaged. Cultures are two-dimensional—one cell layer thick—while biopsies are three-dimensional blocks of tissue; it is hard to freeze a block uniformly.) If the samples were well chosen, they could contain virtually all the genes now present in existing species. In fifty years' time, when the technology that produced Dolly is well advanced and can be extended readily to other species, and when the species that are now endangered are on their last legs and have lost much of their present variation through genetic drift, cells from those frozen cell cultures could be made into Dolly-style embryos, and future creatures could give birth to offspring as diverse as those of today. Since the present-day breeding schemes are so difficult to run and organize (among other things, they require cooperation among people who tend to be highly individualistic), the Dolly technology could offer the most realistic option for many of our best-loved and ecologically most significant wild creatures.

Periodical Bibliography

The following articles have been selected to supplement the diverse views presented in this chapter.

Philip M. Boffey — "Fearing the Worst Should Anyone Produce a Cloned Baby," *New York Times*, January 5, 2003.

Finn Bowring — "Therapeutic and Reproductive Cloning: A Critique," *Social Science & Medicine*, January 15, 2004.

Nathan Gardels — "Cloning: Central Planning of the 21st Century?" *New Perspectives Quarterly*, Fall 2004.

Bob Holmes — "Squeeze Gently to Clone Monkeys," *New Scientist*, December 11, 2004.

Trefor Jenkins — "A Clone of Your Own? The Science and Ethics of Cloning," *British Medical Journal*, August 21, 2004.

Gregory E. Kaebnick — "All Clones Are Not the Same," *New York Times*, January 2, 2003.

Leon R. Kass — "How One Clone Leads to Another," *New York Times*, January 24, 2003.

Charles Krauthammer — "Research Cloning? No," *Washington Post*, May 10, 2002.

William Kristol and Eric Cohen — "A Clone by Any Other Name," *Weekly Standard*, December 23, 2002.

Collin Levey — "Getting to the Root of the Stem-Cell Debate," *Seattle Times*, August 12, 2004.

Rosie Mestel — "Dolly's Death Resurrects Debate on Cloning Ethics," *Los Angeles Times*, February 16, 2003.

Albert Mohler — "Human Cloning in Korea: Does Medicine Have No Moral Limits?" www.crosswalk.com, February 16, 2004.

Edward Rothstein — "The Meaning of 'Human' in Embryonic Research," *New York Times*, March 13, 2004.

Michael J. Sandel — "The Case Against Perfection," *Atlantic Monthly*, April 2004.

Debra J. Saunders — "Parts Is Parts," *San Francisco Chronicle*, June 9, 2004.

Wesley J. Smith — "Cloning and the First State," *Weekly Standard*, January 16, 2004.

Leroy Walters — "Research Cloning, Ethics, and Public Policy," *Science*, March 14, 2003.

Ian Wilmut — "The Limits of Cloning," *BioWorld International*, September 15, 2004.

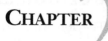

Can Therapeutic Cloning Cure Diseases?

Chapter Preface

The technical term for the procedure of cloning is "somatic cell nuclear transfer." The procedure is the same for animals and humans. The nucleus of a human (or animal) egg is removed (thus removing the egg's DNA) and is replaced with DNA taken from the body tissue (somatic cell) of another individual. With its new somatic cell nucleus, the egg now has a full complement of genes, and it can be manipulated to become an embryo and begin cell division. The embryo can then be implanted in a womb and allowed to develop and be born naturally. The resulting offspring will be genetically identical to the person or animal that supplied the somatic cell that replaced the egg's nucleus. Applied to humans, the use of cloning to produce a child is known as reproductive cloning (although no verified case of a cloned human exists). Alternatively, the embryo can be used for research, a practice known as therapeutic cloning.

Therapeutic cloning involves the use of stem cells from cloned embryos as medical treatments. At a very early stage in the embryo's development, when it is known as a blastocyst and has approximately one hundred cells, its stem cells are harvested and placed in a nutrient medium where they are encouraged to grow. Stem cells are valuable to scientists because they are undifferentiated cells—that is, the cells have not yet begun to specialize—and can therefore be encouraged to grow into any type of body cell. They are also capable of multiplying indefinitely, thus providing a constant source of stem cells (called a stem cell line) to researchers. The theory behind stem cell research is that the stem cells will regenerate the diseased or dying cells in the patient's body. Researchers hope that using stem cells may lead to cures for heretofore incurable, degenerative diseases, such as Parkinson's, Alzheimer's, and juvenile diabetes.

Embryonic stem cell research is controversial because removing the stem cells destroys the embryo in the process. Critics of the research assert that even a single-cell embryo is a human being, and harvesting the embryo's stem cells is tantamount to murder. Supporters of embryonic stem cell research contend that a five- to ten-day-old embryo is not equivalent to a human being and that therefore the research does not destroy a human life. Cloning is not the only source of embryonic stem cells. Such cells can be harvested from embryos left over from in vitro fertilization—embryos that are fated to be destroyed regardless of whether or not they are used for research. Stem cells are also found in umbilical cord blood. Nevertheless, advocates insist that therapeutic cloning is necessary in order to produce embryonic stem cells in sufficient numbers and with the needed characteristics.

Authors in the following chapter debate the merits and demerits of therapeutic cloning.

> *"How'd you like to have your own personal biological repair kit standing by at the hospital? . . . Welcome to the future of medicine."*

Embryonic Stem Cell Research May Save Lives

Ron Reagan

Ron Reagan is the son of former president Ronald R. Reagan who died in 2004 after a long battle with Alzheimer's disease. In the following viewpoint, from a speech he gave at the 2004 Democratic National Convention, he explains why he supports embryonic stem cell research. By taking a small tissue sample from an individual and using cloning technology, he contends, new cells can be created. When these stem cells are inserted back into the individual, they could potentially replace the faulty cells that are responsible for diseases such as Parkinson's and Alzheimer's and could repair spinal cord injuries. Reagan asserts that while embryonic stem cells have the potential to develop into human beings, they are not yet human beings; and therefore their destruction is not unethical.

As you read, consider the following questions:

1. According to Reagan, why do some people object to embryonic stem cell research?
2. How does the author support his contention that embryonic stem cells are not human?

A few of you may be surprised to see someone with my last name showing up to speak at a Democratic convention. Let me assure you, I am not here to make a political speech, and the topic at hand should not—must not— have anything to do with partisanship.

I am here tonight to talk about the issue of research into what may be the greatest medical breakthrough in our or in any lifetime: the use of embryonic stem cells—cells created using the material of our own bodies—to cure a wide range of fatal and debilitating illnesses: Parkinson's disease, multiple sclerosis, diabetes, lymphoma, spinal cord injuries, and much more. Millions are afflicted. Every year, every day, tragedy is visited upon families across the country, around the world.

Now, we may be able to put an end to this suffering. We only need to try. Some of you already know what I'm talking about when I say "embryonic stem cell research." Others of you are probably thinking, hmm, that's quite a mouthful, what is this all about?

The Future of Medicine

Let me try and paint as simple a picture as I can while still doing justice to the incredible science involved. Let's say that ten or so years from now you are diagnosed with Parkinson's disease. There is currently no cure and drug therapy, with its attendant side-effects, can only temporarily relieve the symptoms.

Now, imagine going to a doctor who, instead of prescribing drugs, takes a few skin cells from your arm. The nucleus of one of your cells is placed into a donor egg whose own nucleus has been removed. A bit of chemical or electrical stimulation will encourage your cell's nucleus to begin dividing, creating new cells which will then be placed into a tissue culture. Those cells will generate embryonic stem cells containing only your DNA, thereby eliminating the risk of tissue rejection. These stem cells are then driven to become the very neural cells that are defective in Parkinson's patients.

And finally, those cells—with your DNA—are injected into your brain where they will replace the faulty cells whose failure to produce adequate dopamine led to the Parkinson's disease in the first place.

In other words, you're cured. And another thing, these embryonic stem cells, they could continue to replicate indefinitely and, theoretically, can be induced to recreate virtually any tissue in your body. How'd you like to have your own personal biological repair kit standing by at the hospital? Sound like magic? Welcome to the future of medicine.

Cells Are Not Human Beings

By the way, no fetal tissue is involved in this process. No fetuses are created, none destroyed. This all happens in the laboratory at the cellular level.

Now, there are those who would stand in the way of this remarkable future, who would deny the federal funding so crucial to basic research. They argue that interfering with the development of even the earliest stage embryo, even one that will never be implanted in a womb and will never develop into an actual fetus, is tantamount to murder. A few of these folks, needless to say, are just grinding a political axe and they should be ashamed of themselves. But many are well-meaning and sincere. Their belief is just that, an article of faith, and they are entitled to it.

Markstein. © 2001 by the *Milwaukee Journal Sentinel*. Reproduced by permission of Copley News Service.

But it does not follow that the theology of a few should be allowed to forestall the health and well-being of the many. And how can we affirm life if we abandon those whose own lives are so desperately at risk?

It is a hallmark of human intelligence that we are able to make distinctions. Yes, these cells could theoretically have the potential, under very different circumstances, to develop into human beings—that potential is where their magic lies. But they are not, in and of themselves, human beings. They have no fingers and toes, no brain or spinal cord. They have no thoughts, no fears. They feel no pain. Surely we can distinguish between these undifferentiated cells multiplying in a tissue culture and a living, breathing person—a parent, a spouse, a child.

I know a child—well, she must be 13 now—I'd better call her a young woman. She has fingers and toes. She has a mind. She has memories. She has hopes. And she has juvenile diabetes.

Like so many kids with this disease, she has adjusted amazingly well. The insulin pump she wears—she's decorated hers with rhinestones. She can insert her own catheter needle. She has learned to sleep through the blood drawings in the wee hours of the morning. She's very brave. She is also quite bright and understands full well the progress of her disease and what that might ultimately mean: blindness, amputation, diabetic coma. Every day, she fights to have a future.

We Must Not Fail Our Future

What excuse will we offer this young woman should we fail her now? What might we tell her children? Or the millions of others who suffer? That when given an opportunity to help, we turned away? That facing political opposition, we lost our nerve? That even though we knew better, we did nothing?

And, should we fail, how will we feel if, a few years from now, a more enlightened generation should fulfill the promise of embryonic stem cell therapy? Imagine what they would say of us who lacked the will.

No, we owe this young woman and all those who suffer— we owe ourselves—better than that. We are better than that. A wiser people, a finer nation. And for all of us in this fight, let me say: we will prevail.

The tide of history is with us. Like all generations who have come before ours, we are motivated by a thirst for knowledge and compelled to see others in need as fellow angels on an often difficult path, deserving of our compassion. . . .

We have a chance to take a giant stride forward for the good of all humanity. We can choose between the future and the past, between reason and ignorance, between true compassion and mere ideology. This is our moment, and we must not falter.

> *"It would probably take* about 100 human eggs per patient *to make just one viable cloned embryonic-stem-cell line for use in 'therapeutic cloning.'"*

Embryonic Stem Cell Research Is Impractical

Wesley J. Smith

In the following viewpoint, Wesley J. Smith contends that embryonic stem cell research is not the cure-all that its supporters claim. According to Smith, embryonic stem cell research would require an enormous number of human eggs at tremendous cost. In addition, embryonic stem cells have been found to develop tumors in animals. Smith concludes that adult stem cells show better promise in stem cell research. Smith is a senior fellow at the Discovery Institute think tank and a special consultant to the Center for Bioethics and Culture, an organization that works to educate the public about the ethical issues raised by advances in biotechnology.

As you read, consider the following questions:

1. According to Smith, what is the rationale for cloning embryos offered by its proponents?
2. Why are investors hesitant to find therapeutic cloning ventures in the author's opinion?
3. What alternative to embryonic stem cell therapy does the author advocate?

Ian Wilmut, co-creator of Dolly the cloned sheep, wants your tax dollars to pay Big Biotech and their business partners in elite university life-science departments to conduct research into human cloning. Wilmut dropped this little *bon mot* to the London *Telegraph* while on his way to the United Nations to lobby against a pending international protocol that would outlaw all human-somatic-cell nuclear transfer (SCNT) cloning. He took the opportunity of being interviewed to grouse that America's refusal to publicly fund research into human cloning is stifling science and slowing the development of new medical cures.

Wilmut's complaint is part of an intense public-relations campaign intended to pressure federal and state governments to publicly fund human cloning. Yet only three years ago, during the great stem-cell debate of 2001, biotech advocates assured a wary nation that they only wanted taxpayers to pay for embryonic-stem-cell research (ESCR) that would be strictly limited to using embryos leftover from in-vitro-fertilization treatments. After a protracted political struggle, President [George W.] Bush partially accommodated the request by allowing federal funding on embryonic stem-cell lines already in existence as of August 9, 2001.

The Issue Changes

But now, we are being told that ESCR alone won't lead to treatments for degenerative diseases and disabilities such as Parkinson's, spinal-cord injury, Lou Gehrig's disease, juvenile diabetes, and the like. It seems that our bodies might reject tissues developed from natural embryos. Indeed, according to Robert Lanza, medical director of Advanced Cell Technology, writing in the May 24 [2004] *Scientific American*, the rejection issue is so huge that biotechnologists would require "millions of discarded embryos from IVF clinics" to create stem-cell lines with sufficient genetic variations to mitigate the problem through tissue matching.

Cloning proponents like Lanza claim that the solution to the tissue-rejection conundrum is to make a cloned embryo of each patient and extract the clone's stem cells for use in treatment, a process often called "therapeutic cloning." In theory, since the patient and the clone's DNA would be virtually identical, injected embryonic tissues would not be rejected and the patient would be spared from a lifetime of taking immune suppressant drugs.

Investors Are Hesitant

If Lanza is right and cloning in fact leads to cures for hundreds of millions of people with degenerative conditions worldwide, there would seem to be no limit to the financial profits to be made in this area. Yes, investing in such research would be risky since human cloning is far from perfected. But venture capitalists have been taking substantial risks on biotechnological research for years now: According to the May 20, [2004] *Wall Street Journal*, investors have already poured $100 billion into the biotechnology industry even though $40 billion has been lost. Hence, even if therapeutic cloning is a long shot, cloning companies should still have to beat investors away with a stick.

But the contrary is true. According to several recent news articles, biotech companies hoping to strike it rich via human cloning are withering on the financial vine. It isn't that private capitalists necessarily have moral qualms about human cloning, though they should. More likely, their due diligence has convinced them that therapeutic cloning would be so wildly impractical and expensive to administer that investing money into developing the technology makes about as much financial sense as putting cash through a paper shredder.

The Problems with Therapeutic Cloning

These problems are many and varied, and most seem intractable. They include:

• *The human-egg dearth:* Each attempt at somatic-cell nuclear transfer cloning requires one human egg. (In theory, animal eggs might also be used, but that would create human/animal combinations that in addition to being morally objectionable could also increase the likelihood of rejection.) The National Academy of Sciences has estimated that there are at least 100 million people in America alone that could benefit from stem-cell therapies. Even if it only took one egg per patient, that would still be 100 million eggs. But it is utterly unrealistic to think that cloning will ever become that ef-

Good Ends Do Not Justify Wrong Means

There may be occasions in life when the only means available for achieving a desired end is a means that it would be wrong to employ. This is especially true in circumstances such as those considered here; for to give our initial approval to cloning for biomedical research is to set foot on a path whose deepest implications can scarcely be calculated. People sometimes imagine that human beings are responsible for all the harms they could prevent but do not; yet, this cannot be true. When we refuse to achieve a good outcome by doing what is wrong, and thereby perhaps accept some suffering that might have been avoided, we are not guilty of causing that suffering. To say otherwise would mean that sufficiently evil men could always hold us morally hostage. In order to obligate us to do an evil deed, they need only credibly threaten to do great harm unless we comply. Were we actually responsible for all the harm we might have prevented but did not, they would have us in their moral power. If our duty to prevent harm and suffering were always overriding, if it always held moral trump, we could not live nobly and justly.

We are not deaf to the voices of those who desperately want biomedical research to proceed. Indeed, we can feel the force of that desire ourselves, for all of us—and those we love most—are or could one day be patients desperate for a cure. But we are not only patients or potential patients. We are human beings and citizens, and we know that relief of suffering, though a great good, is not the greatest good. As highly as we value health and longer life, we know that life itself loses its value if we care only for how long we live, and not also for how we live.

The President's Council on Bioethics, *Issues in Law & Medicine*, April 2003.

---

ficient. Indeed, an article published [in 2003] . . . by the NAS (written by Peter Mombaerts of Rockefeller University) revealed that it would probably take *about 100 human eggs per patient* to make just one viable cloned embryonic-stem-cell line for use in "therapeutic cloning." If true, this means we would need a mind-boggling *10 billion eggs* just to treat 100 million Americans—never mind the hundreds of millions of patients who would clamor for such care in the rest of the world. These staggering numbers almost certainly doom therapeutic cloning from ever entering medicine's armamentarium.

• *The unaffordable expense:* The pro-cloning Mombaerts

had more bad news for therapeutic-cloning proponents. At present, young women sell their eggs for use in fertility treatments for $1000 to $2000 each. Given this price, he concluded that the cost of obtaining *one cloned human-embryonic-stem-cell line*—not including the expenses associated with doctors, hospitals, laboratories, etc.—would run in the neighborhood of $200,000 *just for the eggs*, "a prohibitively high sum" that he predicted "will impede the widespread application of this technology in its present form." Even this cost-prohibitive estimate is wildly understated because it doesn't take into account the exponential increase in demand for eggs that therapeutic cloning would cause. Thus, rather than filling investors' coffers, therapeutic cloning would be far more likely to bust the bank.

• *The problem of tumors:* Embryonic stem cells often cause tumors in animal studies, making their use in humans highly problematic. Therapeutic cloning would do nothing to solve this significant safety problem.

Adult-Stem-Cell Research

• *The advances in adult-stem-cell research:* Meanwhile, research into harnessing non-embryonic sources of stem cells for use in medical therapies is advancing at an astounding pace, both in animal studies and early human trials. Human patients with neurological conditions, heart disease, and other illnesses such as sickle-cell anemia, have received substantial benefit in early human trials. Late stage juvenile diabetes in mice has been cured completely using human spleen cells. On June 1 [2004], Johns Hopkins Kimmel Cancer Center announced that bone-marrow stem cells helped rebuild damaged livers in mice. Recently, the *European Journal of Neuroscience* reported that dental pulp provides great support for nerve cells lost to Parkinson's. In Lisbon, Portugal, Dr. Carlos Lima has helped restore some muscular and bladder control to paralyzed patients using olfactory nerve cells. If such breakthroughs continue at the current pace— and if no significant safety issues develop to stand in the way—within the decade embryonic sources for use in stem-cell therapy might become superfluous.

Venture capitalists have no duty to risk their money on

technology that almost surely will never return a profit. Just because this starves Big Biotech of funds to pay for human cloning doesn't mean that society is obliged to fill the gap. Indeed, engaging in such blatant corporate welfare could actually delay viable medical therapies from reaching the medical marketplace, particularly if we divert funds that would otherwise have gone to adult-stem-cell research, which venture capitalists *are* investing in and which is already bringing such great hope to human patients.

"Studying which genes are 'turned off' or 'turned on' in embryonic stem cells derived from a patient with a specific disease . . . could provide insight into how cancers . . . develop."

Therapeutic Cloning Shows Great Promise in Curing Diseases

Robert R. Rich

Therapeutic cloning is one of the most promising tools researchers have for developing therapies for treating diseases, argues Robert R. Rich in the following viewpoint. Stem cells can transform themselves into nerve, heart, brain, or other cell types that could replace damaged tissue. Stem cell research also allows scientists to study the growth of human diseases, such as cancer. However, this research is threatened by politicians who, confused by the difference between therapeutic and reproductive cloning, want to ban all types of cloning. Rich is the executive associate dean of the Emory University School of Medicine and the president of the Federation of American Societies for Experimental Biology.

As you read, consider the following questions:
1. What are totipotent stem cells, as defined by the author?
2. What are some of the diseases that could be cured by totipotent stem cell research, according to Rich?
3. According to Rich, how may scientists begin to understand the genetic basis of a disease?

R ecent dramatic advances in medical research have improved our understanding of human health and are reducing disease, alleviating pain and extending millions of lives. Today, some of the most promising research to extend these gains is imperiled by politics.

This politics either does not understand or does not take into account the differences between cloning to produce a human body—an idea as abhorrent to responsible scientists as to the vast majority of Americans—and the technique of nuclear transplantation to produce stem cells, which is often referred to as "therapeutic cloning." The U.S. Senate soon will consider legislation that would lump these two extraordinarily different approaches together and thus ban some of the most vital and promising biomedical research in our times [the legislation never went to a vote].

Therapeutic Cloning

The technique transplants the nucleus containing the genetic material from an individual's own body cell—such as a skin cell—into an egg cell lacking a nucleus in order to produce totipotent stem cells. Some of the most promising research on human health involves totipotent stem cells, undifferentiated cells that can become almost any type of cell in the body.

In principle, the product of such cells, upon differentiation in a tissue culture dish could become the nerve cells or heart cells or any other cell type that, upon transplantation to the cell donor, might repair or replace a diseased tissue.

Right now, totipotent stem cell research offers hope to millions of Americans suffering from spinal cord injuries or diseases such as heart failure, diabetes, Parkinson's and Alzheimer's. To give just one example of the promise of this research, scientists are exploring how to stimulate stem cells to produce insulin-producing pancreatic islet cells that, when injected into patients, might cure diabetes. But currently researchers are using stem cells from nongenetically identical donors, and this has a drawback: We must learn how to prevent these cells from being rejected by patients who receive them in transplants.

Stem cells produced through nuclear transplantation may

save lives by allowing scientists and physicians to perform transplants while avoiding tissue rejection. The procedure would use the nucleus of a patient's own cell to produce a genetically identical stem cell line for his or her individualized therapy. Medical therapies developed in such a manner should reduce the likelihood of tissue rejection and the need for immunosuppressive drugs.

A Powerful Tool

In addition to the hope of individualized therapies, totipotent stem cells produced using nuclear transplantation also represent a powerful tool for scientists to study human disease. Each cell with a nucleus in the human body contains a full complement of all the genes, but in the process of development and specialization of tissues, some genes are activated and others turned off. Because totipotent stem cells are undifferentiated, these cells have the potential to become virtually any cell type in the body.

Cloning Could Treat Many Diseases

Cloning shows great promise in assisting the treatment of a wide range of diseases such as Parkinson's, Huntington's, Alzheimer's and various cancers, as well as providing more reliable techniques for tissue repair and organ replacement. Many of the treatments envisioned will be applied prior to implanting an embryo, while others can be used at other stages throughout the human life cycle. In addition, cloning techniques could be used in conjunction with other technologies for preventing undesirable genetic traits, or enhancing desirable ones, in offspring. In each instance human embryos and stem cells will be required at least initially, in conducting the research and perfecting the treatments.

Brent Waters, www.science-spirit.org.

By studying which genes are "turned off" or "turned on" in embryonic stem cells derived from a patient with a specific disease, scientists may be able to understand the genetic basis of that disease. For example, this could provide insight into how cancers, which are essentially diseases of unregulated cell growth, develop. Such knowledge could then be applied to preventing disease.

There is overwhelming support in the Senate and in the scientific community for a ban on human cloning for reproductive purposes. The creation of a human being by performing nuclear transplantation and then implanting that clone into a woman's womb is morally wrong—and is opposed by all responsible scientists. But in its rush to ban human reproductive cloning, the Senate may also ban the use of nuclear transplantation to produce stem cells and all of its therapeutic and scientific promise.

Sen. Zell Miller (D-Ga.) is a strong supporter of allowing this important research to continue. The senator's position is admirable, and he is in good company.

Many universities, patient groups and scientific societies, including the Federation of the American Societies for Experimental Biology, the largest coalition of biomedical research scientists in the United States, share support for this vital research.

The opportunities for biomedical research have never been more promising. We must not allow indiscriminate use of the term cloning to prevent us from exploring the possibility that cures for some of our most devastating diseases lie within our own cells.

> *"Therapeutic cloning is a colossal sham designed to draw crucial research resources down a fruitless path with no end in sight."*

Therapeutic Cloning May Not Cure Diseases

Jim Kelly

Jim Kelly was paralyzed with a spinal cord injury in 1997 and has dedicated his life since then to finding a cure for his disability. In the following viewpoint, Kelly maintains that Americans are being misled about the possibilities of therapeutic cloning. The use of stem cells to repair tissue in humans could lead to the development of malignant tumors, he warns. In addition, Kelly insists that advocates of therapeutic cloning have exaggerated the potential of stem cells to avoid immune rejection. He concludes that therapeutic cloning research wastes valuable funds that could be better spent developing other, more promising therapies for spinal cord injuries.

As you read, consider the following questions:

1. In the author's opinion, what is partially responsible for causing birth defects, stunted growth, and premature death in cloning experiments?
2. According to Rudolf Jaenisch, as cited by Kelly, when would therapeutic cloning be safe for treating illnesses?
3. Why might stem cells derived from therapeutic cloning be rejected by the recipient, according to Kelly?

Americans are being misled to their suffering and death for the sake of commercial, scientific, and political agendas.

A Campaign of Misinformation

A non-stop campaign of misinformation and ungrounded hype claims America's best hope for cures lay in "therapeutic" cloning. I'm paralyzed from the chest down, with my life and dreams depending on the successful, efficient use of medical research resources. So it's *not* in my interests to grab at straws instead of looking at scientifically proven facts. The facts are these:

• Cloning of any type, including "therapeutic" cloning or SCNT [somatic cell nuclear transfer], results in widespread, unpredictable genetic flaws on multiple levels in *every* stem cell it aims to create. One of these flaws, called imprinting errors, has been shown in peer-reviewed studies to form malignant tumors when embryonic stem cells with imprinting defects were injected into adult mice. In speaking of this *single* genetic hurdle, the creator of Dolly the Sheep says:

"It should keep a lot of us in business for a long time."

Yet this very issue is *partially* responsible for reproductive cloning causing birth defects, stunted growth, and premature death. And because of this *single* hurdle, MIT [Massachusetts Institute of Technology] Genetic Researcher Rudolf Jaenisch admits he believes *reproductive* cloning can "never" be made to be safe. Apparently Dr. Jaenisch feels *therapeutic* cloning can be safe if Cancer is cured, because the two go hand in hand.

• Cloning is being promoted as a means of avoiding immune rejection of transplanted cells. This is totally false. Experts have known all along that cloning will not reliably avoid rejection. Cells derived from cloning (SCNT) do *not* perfectly match their donor, as is widely misrepresented, because mitochondria of cloning-derived stem cells come from the egg. And these mitochondria contain the egg's DNA. In testifying to the President's Council on Bioethics, Dr. John Gearhart of Johns Hopkins said there was "no question" in his mind that embryonic stem cells derived from cloning "could be rejected. Absolutely." Stanford's Irv Weissman explained:

"I should say that when you put the nucleus in from a somatic cell, the mitochondria still come from the host (the egg)." He concluded, "And in mouse studies it is clear that those genetic differences can lead to a mild but certainly effective transplant rejection and so immunosuppression, mild though it is, will be required for that."

A Doomed Treatment

Hype . . . that has pervaded discussions of therapeutic cloning over the last few years. But now, cold reality is setting in. Biotech researchers and cloning advocates are admitting difficulties in their professional journals, if not yet in the popular press, that make therapeutic cloning look more like a pipe dream than a realistic hope.

Consider a paper by Peter Mombaerts of Rockefeller University, "Therapeutic Cloning in the Mouse," . . . published by the National Academy of Sciences (NAS). Mombaerts has been investigating therapeutic cloning techniques in mice. It has been tough going. Of these efforts, he sadly reports, "The efficiency, or perhaps better, the lack of efficiency thereof, is remarkably consistent." It takes about 100 tries to obtain one viable cloned mouse embryonic stem cell line.

Mombaerts notes that creating human cloned embryos using "nuclear transfer is unlikely to be much more efficient" than it is in mice, especially given that "the efficiency of nuclear transfer has not increased over the years in any of the mammalian species cloned."

If it takes 100 or more tries to make a single human cloned embryonic stem cell line, therapeutic cloning is all but doomed as a viable future medical treatment.

Wesley J. Smith, *National Right to Life News*, October 2003.

More recently Gearhart said that cloning may not be the savior of embryonic stem-cell therapies after all.

"I don't know that nuclear transfer (cloning) is going to be the answer to getting around the immune response question."

Instead he believes that researchers should engineer stem cells that would avoid immune rejection in larger numbers of people, because tailor-made treatments (through cloning) would be too expensive.

The simple truth is that therapeutic cloning is a colossal sham designed to draw crucial research resources down a fruitless path with no end in sight. Before we travel this barren path we already know it won't lead to the "promise" being primarily used to justify our taking a single unnecessarily step: avoiding immune rejection.

Furthermore, we know without a doubt that cloning adds massive *genetic* problems to those inherently involved when implanting embryonic cells in adult tissues. Since these defects *include* (but are by no means *limited* to) the misexpression of genes known to control early embryonic development and the unfolding of the genetic code, one can't help questioning the credibility of claims that cloning "might" reliably provide material to study genetic defects. However, without a doubt, "therapeutic" cloning will eventually provide genetically defective, *un*matched cells needing decades of "astronomically" expensive research (according to Stem Cell Pioneer Dr. John Thomson) to explore their *problems* before any clinical "promise" can safely be addressed.

For the sake of cures, truth, and humanity, please send the message that America's sick and disabled are much more than fodder for the advancement of commercial and research agendas under the *pretext* of looking for cures. Refute the therapeutic cloning lie, don't clone it.

Periodical Bibliography

The following articles have been selected to supplement the diverse views presented in this chapter.

Patrick Dobson "Stem Cell Dilemma: Do Potential Benefits of Research Outweigh Ethical Risks?" *National Catholic Reporter*, June 18, 2004.

Steven Goldberg "Cloning Matters: How *Lawrence v. Texas* Protects Therapeutic Research," *Yale Journal of Health Policy, Law and Ethics*, Summer 2004.

Mark J. Hanson "Cloning for Therapeutic Purposes: Ethical and Policy Considerations," *University of Toledo Law Review*, Spring 2001.

Eve Herold "Stem Cells and the New Future of Medicine," *USA Today*, March 2003.

James Kelly "Cloning: Between Hype and Hope," *Manitou Magazine*, Winter 2004.

Anthony L. Komaroff and George Q. Daley "View from the Lab: Harnessing Stem Cells: Insights from Harvard Medical School," *Newsweek*, December 6, 2004.

Charles Krauthammer, Michael West, and Morton Kondracke "Will Therapeutic Cloning Fail or Foster Future Aging Research?" www.SageCross roads.net, April 23, 2003.

Michael D. Lemonick "Cloning Gets Closer: How a Team Cloned Human Cells to Fight Disease—and Why That's Revolutionary," *Time*, February 23, 2004.

Ricki Lewis "Mike West: Cloning for Human Therapeutics," *Scientist*, September 16, 2002.

Carlos Lima "Human Olfactory Mucosa Grains in Traumatic Spinal Cord Injuries: A Way to Cure Paralysis?" *Brainland Neuroscience Information Centre*, March 13, 2002.

James Meek "Baby Cord Cells Offer Leukaemia Breakthrough," *Guardian*, July 9, 2002.

President's Council on Bioethics "The Moral Case Against Cloning for Biomedical Research," *Issues in Law & Medicine*, April 2003.

Debashis Singh "Human Cloning Is Justified in Preventing Genetic Disease," *British Medical Journal*, February 28, 2004.

Wesley J. Smith "An Indecent Proposition," *Weekly Standard*, October 18, 2004.

Gretchen Vogel "Scientists Take Step Toward Therapeutic Cloning," *Science*, February 13, 2004.

Ian Wilmut "The Moral Imperative for Human Cloning," *New Scientist*, February 21, 2004.

CHAPTER 3

Should Researchers Use Adult or Embryonic Stem Cells?

Chapter Preface

Until the turn of the twenty-first century, embryonic stem cells were the only cells being studied and used in stem cell research. Then in 2002, Catherine Verfaillie, the director of the Stem Cell Institute at the University of Minnesota and a doctor who specializes in hematology and oncology, published the results of her research on adult stem cells and inadvertently started a raging and bitter controversy over stem cell research.

Verfaillie's important discovery was that multipotent stem cells can be found in human adults. Such cells, previously thought to be present only in embryos, have the ability to develop into various different specialized cells. This characteristic makes them much more promising than typical, "differentiated" cells as potential cures for diseases. Verfaillie cultured cells from an adult's bone marrow and ended up with not only bone, cartilage, and fat cells—which were expected—but also with brain, liver, and endothelial cells (cells that line the blood vessels)—which were not expected. In a *New Scientist* article announcing the results of Verfaillie's research, writer Sylvia Pagan Westphal calls the type of cell Verfaillie discovered the "ultimate stem cell" and "the most important cell ever discovered." Westphal adds that with proper growing conditions, the adult stem cells—like embryonic stem cells—can transform themselves into muscle, cartilage, bone, and liver tissues, as well as neurons and brain cells.

When Verfaillie published her findings, she did not expect the swirl of controversy that would come to surround her work. Critics of embryonic stem cell research argue that embryonic research should be discontinued since adult stem cells appear to have all of the advantages of embryonic stem cells and do not require destroying a potential human life. David Prentice, a senior fellow with the conservative Family Research Council, has testified before Congress, urging it to ban all embryonic stem cell research. He maintains that stem cell research can continue using adult stem cells instead of embryonic stem cells.

However, supporters of embryonic stem cell research, and even Verfaillie herself, contend that it is premature to discontinue embryonic stem cell research. Other scientists have been unable to duplicate Verfaillie's bone marrow experiments, they point out, while embryonic stem cells have been differentiating into all kinds of tissues for more than twenty years. Leonard Zon, president of the International Society for Stem Cell Research, argues that both embryonic and adult stem cell research are needed. "Advances in one field help the other," he asserts.

In the following chapter, authors present their arguments for and against embryonic and adult stem cell research.

"It is an incontrovertible fact that embryonic stem cells have the ability to form all cells in the body."

Embryonic Stem Cell Research Is More Promising than Adult Stem Cell Research

George Daley

Opponents of embryonic stem cell research contend that the embryos used in such research, whether they are created through cloning or fertility treatments, are fully human. Rather than destroy embryos to extract stem cells, these critics advocate the use of adult stem cells. In the following viewpoint —an excerpt of his testimony before a U.S. Senate committee on embryonic stem cell research—George Daley asserts that while the research on adult stem cells is promising, it is not so promising that research should be abandoned on embryonic stem cells. Adult stem cells do not exist for all tissues of the human body, he insists, whereas embryonic stem cells can become any type of tissue. George Daley is an associate professor of pediatrics and biological chemistry at Boston Children's Hospital and Harvard Medical School and the associate director of the Children's Hospital Stem Cell Program.

As you read, consider the following questions:
1. How does Daley describe the opponents and supporters of embryonic stem cell research?
2. In Daley's view, those who claim that the study of adult stem cells should trump the study of embryonic stem cells are a part of what group?

George Daley, testimony before the U.S. Senate Committee on Commerce, Science, and Transportation, Washington, DC, September 29, 2004.

I am a physician-scientist, board certified in Internal Medicine and Hematology and clinically active in the care of children and adults with malignant and genetic diseases of the blood and bone marrow. I run an NIH-supported[1] laboratory that studies both adult and embryonic stem cells. Part of my lab focuses on the human disease Chronic Myeloid Leukemia, a cancer that arises from the adult blood stem cell. Part of my lab is investigating how to coax embryonic stem cells to differentiate into blood stem cells. My laboratory has succeeded in transplanting mice with blood stem cells derived entirely in vitro from embryonic stem cells. Our goal is to replicate this success using human embryonic stem cells, with the hope of someday treating patients with leukemia, immune deficiency, aplastic anemia, and genetic diseases like sickle cell anemia. . . .

Surrounded by Controversy

Controversy surrounds the field of human embryonic stem cell research. At the core of the controversy is the fact that harvesting embryonic stem cells requires the destruction of a human embryo. If you ascribe full personhood to the earliest stages of human development, then you are vigorously opposed to embryonic stem cell research and opposed to fertility treatments that generate embryos that are the source of embryonic stem cells. In contrast, if you believe that the earliest human embryos, as microscopic balls of primitive cells, are not the moral equivalents of babies, then you are likely to be equally vigorous in supporting embryonic stem cell research because of its immense promise for understanding and treating disease. These dueling perspectives are informed more by religious and moral beliefs than by scientific principles. However, scientific issues indeed play an important role in the current debate. As with most controversies, much misinformation exists. Today, I am here to offer scientific testimony to clarify the facts and dispel the myths surrounding competing claims in adult and embryonic stem cell research.

I will address two central scientific questions: First, is re-

1. The National Institutes of Health (NIH) is the federal government's medical research agency.

search on human adult stem cells so promising that we need not pursue research with embryonic stem cells? Second, is the [Bush administration] policy that restricts researchers to only a limited set of cell lines created before August 9th, 2001 adequate to explore the potential of human embryonic stem cell research?

Misinformation About Stem Cell Research

The misinformation surrounding stem cell research has had a damaging impact on the creation of public policy. For example, the idea has been put forward that adult stem cells are better than embryonic stem cells because they have the same therapeutic potential without the controversy. The fact is that stem cells from fertilized eggs have the ability to grow into any type of cell or organ in the body. Adult tissue stem cells appear to have a much more restricted path for development, limiting their usefulness in therapies for diseases. Recently 80 Nobel Laureates sent a letter to President [George W.] Bush stating that, "it is premature to conclude that adult stem cells have the same potential as embryonic stem cells." The Department of Health and Human Services released a report, "Stem Cells: Scientific Progress and Future Research Directions," in June 2001. The report confirms the incredible potential that embryonic stem cells represent. It also stresses that there is limited evidence that adult stem cells can generate mature, fully functional cells or that the cells have restored lost function in vivo.

Christopher Reeve, testimony before the New Jersey Senate Health, Human Services, and Senior Citizens Committee, November 25, 2002.

The simple but emphatic answer to the first question is "no." Although research on adult stem cells is enormously promising and has already yielded clinical success in the form of bone marrow transplantation, adult stem cells are not the biological equivalents of embryonic stem cells, and adult stem cells will not satisfy all scientific and medical needs. Moreover, a great many questions about adult stem cells remain unanswered. Adult stem cells have been unequivocally isolated from bone marrow, skin, and mesenchyme, but adult stem cells do not appear to exist for all tissues of the body. Claims of stem cells for the heart, pancreas, and kidney remain controversial. You will also hear claims that adult stem cells are plastic, perhaps as versatile as embryonic stem cells, and that success with adult stem cells obviates the need to study embryonic stem cells. As an expert in both adult and embryonic stem cell biology, I take issue with these claims. It is the nature of adult stem cells to regenerate only a limited subset of the body's tissues. As best we can tell, under normal physiologic circumstances, adult stem cells do not have a measurable capacity to differentiate beyond their tissue of origin. Therefore, asking blood stem cells to regenerate heart or liver or brain is to ask adult stem cells to betray their intrinsic nature. Like cellular alchemy, attempts to engineer adult stem cell plasticity may never succeed in a clinically practical manner. I am not arguing we should not invest in some highly speculative realms of cellular engineering with adult stem cells. Indeed, we should. I am arguing however, that the promise of adult stem cells in no way obviates the need to investigate embryonic stem cells. Claiming that the study of adult stem cells should trump the study of embryonic stem cells is an opinion at the fringe and not the forefront of scientific thinking.

While the differentiation spectrum of adult stem cells is restricted, it is an incontrovertible fact that embryonic stem cells have the ability to form all cells in the body. Such is the natural endowment of the stem cells of the early embryo, and the very reason they inspire such fascination among stem cell biologists. Scientists are seeking to discover the natural mechanisms that drive formation of specific cells and tissues, so that these principles can be faithfully reproduced with embryonic stem cells in the Petri dish. I would argue that coaxing embryonic stem cells to do what comes naturally to them is more likely to prove successful in the near term than reengineering adult stem cells towards unnatural ends. The American Society of Cell Biology and every other major scientific society supports the study of both adult and embryonic stem cells.

Missed Opportunities

To the second question, "Is the current Presidential policy adequate to explore the potential of human embryonic stem cell research?" I also answer an emphatic "no." Today, federally-funded scientists operate under a restrictive policy that limits the human embryonic stem cells that can be studied to a modest number of lines generated over three years ago. With the pre-2001 vintage cell lines we can address generic questions, but are prohibited from exploiting the latest tools being developed around the Globe. It runs contrary to the American spirit of innovation for our government to deny its scientists every advantage to push the frontiers. Ultimately this will slow the pace of medical research, and compromise the next generation of medical breakthroughs. I recently published an article in the *New England Journal of Medicine* entitled "Missed opportunities in human embryonic stem cell research", in which I articulated the scientific avenues that are not being adequately investigated due to the current Presidential policy. In the three years since the President announced his policy, over a hundred additional lines have been generated, many with advantageous properties that make them highly valuable to medical scientists. Some of these new lines model diseases like cystic fibrosis, muscular dystrophy, and genetic forms of mental retardation. What does the President say to families whose children are affected by these devastating diseases? How does the President justify his lack of support for this research? Where is the compassion in such a policy?

Thankfully, I am the father of two healthy boys, ages 3 and 6. I am taking great delight in teaching them baseball and watching them root for the Red Sox. . . . As a father, I count my blessings for these God-given gifts, more so every time I walk through the lobby of the Children's Hospital, and see the many kids who will never run the bases or smack a home run. As a physician, I see the mission of ES [embryonic stem] cell research as providing the greatest hope to relieve the suffering I see in many of my patients. As a scientist, I am not impervious to the expressions of ethical concern for the sanctity of the human embryo. But in our religiously plural society, I fear we may never reach an ethical consensus given the competing entities in this debate: microscopic human embryos that represent incipient human life on the one hand, desperate patients suffering from debilitating diseases on the other. From my perspective as a father, physician, and scientist, I am moved by concern for my two boys, my patients, and for the life-affirming mission of hope and promise in embryonic stem cell research.

> *"Adult stem cells, which can be obtained from a person's own body . . ., are already showing far greater promise of delivering cures for a range of conditions."*

Adult Stem Cell Research Is More Promising than Embryonic Stem Cell Research

Carolyn Moynihan

In the following viewpoint, Carolyn Moynihan argues that embryos are human beings in the earliest stage of their lives and that cloning embryos to obtain stem cells for research purposes would be murder. She maintains that there is an alternative to embryonic stem cells, though: adult stem cells, which do not require that human embryos be killed. Moynihan cites instances of adult stem cell treatments that have had encouraging results. Embryonic stem cells, on the other hand, have not been shown to have helped a single patient. Moynihan is a writer specializing in bioethics.

As you read, consider the following questions:
1. In Moynihan's view, what is the difference between embryos that are "surplus products" of in vitro fertilization and embryos cloned solely for research purposes?
2. According to Richard Faull, as quoted by Moynihan, what problems would be overcome by using adult stem cells?
3. What examples does the author give of successful adult stem cell treatments?

In an age dominated by images, important debates are often won by those who pack the greatest visual, and, therefore, emotional punch. A case in point is Christopher "Superman" Reeve, whose advocacy of "therapeutic" cloning carries the considerable moral weight and visual drama of his determination to walk again after paralysis from a spinal-cord injury. [Editor's note: Reeve died in October 2004 from complications due to his paralysis.]

When Reeve gets in front of the camera, . . . and tells us that we must allow the cloning of human embryos to provide stem cells for cures for people like him, when he is surrounded by his family, devoted caregivers and a team of earnest scientists, what can we say? Can there be any problem with cloning that trumps such noble desires and human effort?

Human Lives Are Destroyed

Frankly, yes. Contrary to what Reeve and some scientists say, stem-cell technology using human embryos does involve the destruction of human lives. If they were not human and not alive, they would be useless for the purpose they are supposed to serve: the regeneration of damaged tissues and organs.

It makes no difference whether the embryos are the "surplus products" of IVF [in vitro fertilization] procedures or cloned from a person solely for research and therapeutic uses; they are human beings in the first stage of life and the harvesting of their stem cells kills them. It is not therapeutic for them.

To many people this destructive manipulation of human life is abhorrent. It can be rationalised in various ways but it will always be, at best, controversial, and this is hardly what a good scientist would wish for as the basis for a new generation of therapies.

The Future of Stem-Cell Research

The good news is—and we never seem to hear this from Christopher Reeve and friends—that the future of stem-cell research does not depend on using human embryos. Adult stem cells, which can be obtained from a person's own body (child or adult), are already showing far greater promise of delivering cures for a range of conditions, including spinal-cord injury.

[In early 2003], . . . Professor Richard Faull of the University of Auckland [New Zealand] school of medicine told a conference in Adelaide [Australia] of encouraging results from international research using adult stem cells to repair human brains damaged by diseases such as Huntington's, Parkinson's and Alzheimer's.

Adult Stem Cells Have Enormous Potential

Historically only a few stem cells were recognized in humans. . . . These stem cells were considered to have very limited repertoires, related to replenishment of cells within their tissue of origin. These limitations were considered to be a normal part of the developmental paradigm in which cells become more and more restricted in their lineage capabilities, leading to defined and specific differentiated cells in body tissues. Thus, discovery of stem cells in other tissues, or with the ability to cross typical lineage boundaries, is both exciting and confusing. . . .

Our current knowledge regarding adult stem cells has expanded greatly over what was known just a few short years ago. Results from both animal studies and early human clinical trials indicate that they have significant capabilities for growth, repair, and regeneration of damaged cells and tissues in the body, akin to a built-in repair kit or maintenance crew that only needs activation and stimulation to accomplish repair of damage. The potential of adult stem cells to impact medicine in this respect is enormous.

David A. Prentice, *Issues in Law & Medicine*, Spring 2004.

Professor Faull's comment on the significance of this research is worth quoting: "By tapping into and genetically engineering the adult stem cells from the diseased adult brain, we would overcome major ethical, immunological and technical problems associated with the more controversial area of embryonic stem-cell technology."

This is a scientist speaking, not a religious fanatic, and he acknowledges major ethical problems.

Notice also there are immunological problems with embryo cells. Embryonic stem-cell technology is not merely a question of using "unwanted" IVF embryos, since cells from these injected into patients would be rejected by their immune system.

As Christopher Reeve's campaign makes clear, therapies require making clones of a patient in order to extract compatible stem cells. The problem is, each clone is a new human being.

Promising Results

But remember, we do not in any sense need to do this. Embryonic cells may be more plastic than adult cells but genetic engineering can make the latter adaptable enough, and the results of research so far, as reported in leading scientific journals, are very promising. A few examples:

• German doctors have used a patient's own bone marrow stem cells to regenerate tissue damaged by a heart attack.

• Doctors in the United States have taken stem cells from the brain of a patient with Parkinson's disease and reimplanted them, resulting in an 83 per cent improvement in the patient.

• Melissa Holley, paraplegic as a result of a severed spinal cord, has been treated with her own immune cells and regained movement of her toes, and bladder control.

• In Britain, a boy aged three has been cured of a fatal disease by the use of stem cells extracted from his sister's placenta.

No Results for Embryonic Stem-Cell Research

By contrast, embryonic stem cells have not helped a single patient. What they have done is provide pharmaceutical companies with a useful medium for testing how drugs work—even more useful when the embryo cells are cultured on aborted fetal tissue.

They can refine their products before starting trials on human subjects, thus saving money and shortening the lead time for bringing new drugs on the market.

Private companies and venture capitalists regard stem-cell research aimed at cures for Alzheimer's and diabetes sufferers as far too risky.

Advocates argue it is too risky only because of legal restrictions on embryonic stem-cell research. But those restraints have served to show there is a better way of pursuing stem-cell technology and the wonderful therapies it promises.

I have a sister afflicted with Parkinson's disease, having developed it as a young woman more than 40 years ago. It is a cruel disease and I would love to see a cure for it. But would I want a cure at the price of manufacturing human beings and cannibalising them for body parts? No way.

Good science is ethical science and cures will come from it as they always have. Adult stem-cell research lacks the emotive power of the Reeve factor, but it is the one with runs on the board.

"It's entirely too early to give up on any form of stem cell that might have therapeutic value in the long run."

Both Adult and Embryonic Stem Cells Should Be Used in Research

Bernadine Healy

Embryonic stem cells offer much potential in research to cure diseases, asserts Bernadine Healy in the following viewpoint. However, a great deal of debate surrounds the creation of such stem cells by means of cloning and in vitro fertilization. In the midst of this debate, adult stem cells also show promise in curing disease. While the debate over the ethical implications of creating embryos is resolved, Healy advocates focusing research using adult stem cells and existing human embryos. Healy is a cardiologist and former director of the National Institutes of Health.

As you read, consider the following questions:
1. What is the real issue concerning embryonic stem cells, in Healy's opinion?
2. Why were adult stem cells ignored until recently, according to the author?

Bernadine Healy, "The Other Stem Cells," *U.S. News & World Report*, vol. 136, June 14, 2004, p. 77. Copyright © 2004 by U.S. News & World Report, L.P. Reproduced by permission.

L ike children, human embryonic stem cells are filled with potential but difficult to control. Since they were first isolated in 1998 from human embryos only a few days old, these primordial cells have achieved both fame and notoriety. Removed from their tightly programmed life as an embryo, they can multiply indefinitely in the lab in primitive form or they can be coaxed to differentiate into virtually any cell in the body—a nest of beating heart cells, for example. But inject them into intact animals, and they are just as likely to be rejected by the immune system or turned into a deadly tumor filled with teeth, hair, and random cells.

These untamed primitive cells are important because they're a potential inroad to cures for devastating diseases like Parkinson's, diabetes, heart failure, and Alzheimer's. Their promise has stirred the imagination of the public, ignited the fervor of [former First Lady] Nancy Reagan and others wounded by such illnesses, and attracted piles of money from government, commercial investors, and philanthropists. And the view that embryonic stem cells per se are forbidden fruit —as argued by abortion opponents—may be softening. [In June 2004], . . . over 250 members of Congress, including avowed "pro-lifers," came out in support of using taxpayer money on the estimated 400,000 frozen spare embryos, stored in fertility clinics, that might otherwise be destroyed.

The Real Issue

But all this hoopla fails to confront the real issue, which is not about using spare embryos. Rather it's about giving scientists license to make living human embryos from scratch— through IVF or human cloning—that is part and parcel of the long-term pursuit of therapeutically usable embryonic stem cells. This is the hidden but ever so hot issue on which there is no consensus, either in Congress or among the states. California has a voter referendum in November [2004] to issue a $3 billion bond to support stem-cell research, including therapeutic cloning. [The referendum passed.] Other states have outlawed this approach entirely. Even the European Parliament and the United Nations have failed to agree whether therapeutic cloning is blessed or sinful.

What may be saving embryonic stem cells from the polit-

Potential U.S. Patient Populations for Stem Cell–Based Therapies

High incidence of the following conditions suggests that stem cell research could potentially help millions of Americans.

Condition	Number of Patients	
Cardiovascular disease	58	million
Autoimmune diseases	30	million
Diabetes	16	million
Osteoporosis	10	million
Cancers	8.2	million
Alzheimer's disease	5.5	million
Parkinson's disease	5.5	million
Burns (severe)	0.3	million
Spinal-cord injuries	0.25	million
Birth defects (per year)	0.15	million

The National Academies, "Stem Cells and the Future of Regenerative Medicine," 2002.

ical quagmire are their increasingly compelling distant cousins, adult stem cells, which are quickly making regenerative medicine a dramatic reality. Until recently these cells have been largely ignored because they were thought to have limited regenerative value. But that has changed, in part because of the fuss and money surrounding embryo research. These less primitive but more stable cells exist in small quantities in all body organs. They won't be rejected and won't cause uncontrolled cell growth, and are therefore preferred for patient therapy. Of particular interest are the ones that nest in the bone marrow; they have the ability to transform into almost any tissue in the body.

Network

We are just learning that in the body, adult stem cells are players in a highly disciplined ballet. Indeed, they are key elements in a repair network in which wounded tissue sends out molecular SOS signals that mobilize stem cells in the affected organ and at the same time recruit bone marrow stem cells to home into the injury site. This may lead to a slow but natural replacement of tissues over time. Just last month

[May 2004] a study in *Lancet* from the University of Florida reported that women who had had bone-marrow transplants from male donors were found—at autopsy months to years later—to have low levels of neurons of male origin, i.e., brain cells with Y chromosomes. Similar findings in both humans and animals suggest that stem cells may be replenishing other organs as well. A critical research question is whether or not these self-replenishing powers can be made to work faster and better, perhaps through drugs that stimulate stem-cell multiplication. Research already has some promising results.

Study Both

Does this mean that embryonic stem cells should be abandoned? Absolutely not. They are powerful models for understanding how basic stem cells function. And it's entirely too early to give up on any form of stem cell that might have therapeutic value in the long run. But the meteoric ascent of adult cells as viable options for therapy, and the possibility of more spare embryos for research, together provide breathing room for a much-needed public debate. There remain many unresolved social, ethical, and legal issues regarding the creation of embryos and clones for research. Not the least of these are the potential for exploitation of young women to get fresh eggs for this work and the lack of boundaries for research on embryos when it's conducted privately.

A stem-cell biologist recently quipped to me that our children may live forever because of stem-cell work, but we are certain to die. We don't have forever for this crucial debate.

"It is possible that one day in the near future, hundreds of thousands of Americans will be able to get out of their wheelchairs and walk again. And embryonic stem-cell research could be the reason why."

Embryonic Stem Cell Treatments Could Cure Spinal Cord Injuries

Steve Glassner

Opponents of embryonic stem cell research argue that adult stem cells have the same potential to cure diseases as stem cells that are harvested from embryos created through cloning or fertility treatments. In the following viewpoint Steve Glassner rejects this view. He contends that embryonic stem cells have the ability to form—and potentially replace—any type of cells in the human body, whereas adult stem cells are more limited in the types of tissue they can repair. The stem cells' ability to become any kind of human tissue holds promise for repairing nerve damage in spinal cord injuries, he concludes. Glassner is a writer for *Paraplegia News* and a former intern for the Paralyzed Veterans of America in Washington, D.C.

As you read, consider the following questions:
1. What is the main difference between embryonic and adult stem cells, according to the author?
2. What federal regulation did President Bush establish that served as a compromise in the stem cell debate, according to Glassner?

Steve Glassner, "Fighting Diseases with Cells: Stem-Cell Research: Peril—or Potential?" *Paraplegia News*, vol. 58, September 2004, p. 14. Copyright © 2004 by the Paralyzed Veterans of America. Reproduced by permission.

On May 9, 2004, less than a month before her husband's death, former First Lady Nancy Reagan spoke at the Juvenile Diabetes Research Foundation gala in Los Angeles. That night she received a standing ovation from a crowded ballroom at the Beverly Wilshire Hotel as she was presented with an award by Michael J. Fox. She was being honored for her work in promoting stem-cell research.

"Science has presented us with a hope called stem-cell research," said Mrs. Reagan, "which may provide our scientists with answers that have so long been beyond our grasp. I just don't see how we can turn our backs on this; there are just so many diseases that can be cured, or at least helped. We have lost so much time already, and I just really can't bear to lose any more."

What Are Stem Cells?

Stem cells can replace and replenish other cells within a living organism by continuously dividing without limit. According to the National Institutes of Health (NIH), when a stem cell divides, each new cell has the potential to either remain a stem cell or become another type of cell with a more specialized function, such as a muscle cell, a red blood cell, or a brain cell.

Medical experts and scientists around the world believe stem cells will revolutionize the way we look at life-threatening diseases. They have the potential to cure diseases such as Parkinson's, diabetes, and Alzheimer's—the disease former President Reagan eventually died from. Stem cells even have the possibility of repairing spinal-cord injuries (SCIs), thereby giving hope to people with paraplegia and tetraplegia for the return of functions including walking, bladder and bowel control, and temperature regulation.

In the past decade, funding and support for stem-cell research has gained greater national acceptance. [In 2004], for example, the University of California–San Francisco began developing new stem-cell lines at its new, $11-million private stem-cell research center. In February [2004], Harvard University announced it would raise as much as $100 million to start a stem-cell research institute. And in January [2004], New Jersey joined California in becoming the only two states in the country that allow stem-cell research.

Many individuals in this country, however, do not support stem-cell research because of concern about where these cells come from. The most popular form of stem-cell research is known as embryonic (or pluripotent). This is where research is conducted on stem cells from human embryos that are only a few days old, left over from in vitro fertilization (IVF) procedures. Various pro-life and religious groups, including the National Right to Life Committee and the U.S. Conference of Catholic Bishops, equate research on embryonic stem cells with murder.

The reality is that embryonic stem-cell research only takes place in a Petri dish, and there is no way the human embryo can grow or develop until it is implanted into a woman's uterus. In an editorial in the May 31, 2004, edition of *Time* magazine, Michael Kinsley points out that despite how people feel about the issue of abortion, stem cells are essentially nothing more than "a few dozen cells that together are too small to be seen without a microscope. [They have] no conclusions, no self-awareness, no ability to feel love or pain. The smallest insect is far more human in every respect except potential."

Adult or Embryonic?

Some people who oppose embryonic stem-cell research accept what is known as adult (or multipotent) research, where stem cells are taken from tissue such as bone marrow, brain, muscle, or liver in a born human being. They say adult stem cells are equally as promising—if not more so—than embryonic stem cells. Most scientists, however, disagree with this assertion. They believe the real potential for fighting diseases lies in embryonic stem cells.

Like embryonic stem cells, adult stem cells have the ability to self-renew and can replace damaged tissue. However, they can only replace tissue from specific forms of tissue similar to themselves, whereas embryonic stem cells can form— and potentially replace—cells of any kind of tissue within the body.

Embryonic stem cells have already been used to treat lab mice with diabetes by using beta cells that produce insulin found in the pancreas. According to the June 21, 2004, issue of *Newsweek* magazine, Harvard biologist Doug Melton recently concluded that adult stem cells could not be found in the pancreas. Instead, he insists, "If you want to make more beta cells, the place to look is embryonic stem cells."

Scientists agree there is some promise in adult stem cells. For instance, a person with Alzheimer's disease may one day be able to benefit from a transplant with adult stem cells from a healthy brain. There is also the possibility that a drug will be developed that can initiate the growth of adult stem cells within an individual's own brain to fix the destruction from the Alzheimer's.

But despite the potential, just as much doubt exists about the effectiveness of adult stem cells based on previous research. According to the aforementioned issue of *Newsweek*, results from a 2001 medical study by New York Medical College that purported adult bone-marrow stem cells had become cardiac muscle in mice could not be replicated by other scientists in April 2004 when they tried to validate the study. That same article mentions a 2000 study at the University of Oregon that said adult-blood stem cells were able to turn into liver cells in mice. In 2002, however, the lead researcher on that study came to the conclusion that "the blood cells had fused with the existing liver cells—more a case of biological identity theft than transformation."

President Bush and Research

Though significant disagreement may always exist over the issue of embryonic stem-cell research, in August 2001, President George W. Bush established federal regulations that are a compromise between these two points of view. The regulations allow using federal funds for research upon the 60 stem-cell lines (that number is now 62) that already existed through private research, but prohibited the development of new stem-cell lines. The President explained that under these regulations, the federal government would be able to "explore the promise and potential of stem-cell research without crossing a fundamental moral line by providing taxpayer funding that would sanction or encourage further destruction of human embryos that have at least the potential for life."

President Bush established several conditions for use of federal funds. First, they could only go toward research where there was informed consent of the donors of the embryos. Second, funds could only go toward excess embryos produced solely for reproductive intent. Finally, there must be no financial reward to entice embryo donors to give them up for research. Also, federal funds cannot be used in three areas: (1) derivation or use of stem cells from newly destroyed embryos, (2) creation of embryos for research purposes, and (3) cloning of embryos for any purpose.

Enormous Potential

[A study] has been done on rats with induced spinal cord injuries. Nine days after injury, those rats were treated with embryonic stem cell transplants. After two to five weeks, those rats demonstrated improvement in weight bearing and coordination, and at autopsy they were found to have adult versions of the transplanted fetal cells. If these types of procedures are someday available to humans, their benefit to spinal cord injury patients could be enormous.

American Federation for Aging Research, "The Latest Research on Stem Cell Transplants and Spinal Cord Injury," April 24, 2003.

NIH, the government's top biomedical research organization, is mandated to watch over and execute President Bush's orders. Right after President Bush made this decision, he established a President's Council on Bioethics in order to study the human and moral ramifications of developments in behavioral science and technology. This includes areas such as embryo and stem-cell research, assisted reproduction, cloning, genetic screening, gene therapy, euthanasia, psychoactive drugs, and brain implants. The council was led by Dr. Leon Krass of the University of Chicago.

Pro-Life Support

Despite concern over whether embryonic stem-cell research is appropriate, a sign it is achieving greater acceptance is that it is gaining proponents from unlikely places. In particular, support is coming from several pro-life Republicans in Congress such as former Florida Senator Connie Mack, Oregon Senator Gordon Smith, and Utah Senator Orrin Hatch. In

2001, Hatch, who is Mormon, said he "rarely, if ever, observed such genuine excitement for the prospects of future progress than is presented by embryonic stem-cell research."

Another pro-life Republican supporter of embryonic stem cells is California Congressman Duke Cunningham. He became interested in the issue when a disease-stricken child from his district came up to him and said, "Congressman, you're the only one who can save my life." Cunningham became an official supporter after scientists explained to him that most of the thousands of frozen embryos stored in IVF clinics, the same embryos scientists use for stem-cell research, are otherwise discarded. In his support of embryonic stem-cell research, Cunningham believes he is "actually saving a life from something that is not going to be life" anyway.

Treatment for Spinal-Cord Injury

One significant area of potential for embryonic stem-cell research is the repair of nerve damage in SCI. A primary effect of SCI and other neurological conditions is loss of neurons. When neurons are lost or destroyed, the nerve connections that help control the body are interrupted, and control over certain functions is compromised. Scientists believe embryonic stem cells have the potential of changing into and repairing these neurons.

The loss of glial support cells is another primary effect of SCI. Glial cells are non-neuronal cells that still play a major role in the nervous system by creating myelin, a fatty sheath that coats axons and allows nerve impulses to travel quickly down these nerve fibers. Scientists believe embryonic stem cells, like neuronal cells, have the potential to help produce new glial cells and thus help produce myelin after nerve damage.

Several recent medical experiments with lab mice have already begun to show the potential of stem cells in SCI. In a study published in *Proceedings of the National Academy of Sciences*, scientists at Washington University School of Medicine in St. Louis used stem cells to produce glial cells in the spinal cords of mice. In April 2001, the American Association of Neurological Surgeons conducted a study where certain lab mice with SCI were injected with transplants of stem cells of neural origin, while others with SCI were used as a control. The study found that the mice receiving the transplants showed greater functional healing than did the control mice.

PVA's Stand

The Paralyzed Veterans of America (PVA) supports embryonic stem-cell research because it believes such research has the potential to lead to treatments and possibly cures for devastating SCIs and diseases that result in paralysis. Research supported by this organization must comply with all federal rules according to the policy laid down by President Bush. This support is not a promotion of abortion or of the generation of extra in vitro fertilization embryos specifically for research purposes.

PVA realizes that many moral and religious beliefs revolve around the issue of stem-cell research and respects the views of others. But as Congressman Cunningham said, we are "saving a life from something that is not going to be life."

PVA urges its members and other *Paraplegia News* readers to look at the great potential stem-cell research has to offer for people with SCI. It is possible that one day in the near future, hundreds of thousands of Americans will be able to get out of their wheelchairs and walk again. And embryonic stem-cell research could be the reason why.

"There has been tremendous progress in adult stem cell research in the last few years."

Adult Stem Cell Treatments Are Curing Spinal Cord Injuries

Jean D. Peduzzi-Nelson

The following viewpoint is an excerpt of Jean D. Peduzzi-Nelson's testimony before a U.S. Senate committee hearing on adult stem cell research. She argues that people who promote the use of embryonic stem cells for research—including stem cells derived from cloned embryos—are motivated by the desire to make money. Adult stem cells show much more promise for treating diseases, she contends. For example, patients with spinal cord injuries who received treatments of adult stem cells taken from the patients' nasal passages all showed improvements in muscle mobility, and some showed improvements in other areas as well. Peduzzi-Nelson is a research associate professor who specializes in the development and evaluation of spinal cord treatments at the University of Alabama at Birmingham.

As you read, consider the following questions:
1. What are some alternative treatments to embryonic stem cells, in Peduzzi-Nelson's opinion?
2. According to the author, what happened to the guinea pigs that received a transplant of olfactory mucosa?
3. What is the major advantage of using olfactory mucosa in treatments, in the author's view?

Jean D. Peduzzi-Nelson, testimony before the U.S. Senate Committee on Commerce, Science, and Transportation, Washington, DC, July 14, 2004.

S ome people naively think that the stem cell controversy is just related to the abortion issue, political party alignment, religious beliefs, or scientific freedom. However, none of these are the driving force in the effort to promote Federal funding of human embryonic stem cells or human cloning. The most profitable, not the best, treatment for people is being promoted. The main reason for the current emphasis on human embryonic stem cells and cloning is money. The old statement of 'follow the money' explains many of the statements made regarding this controversy. It is a superior business plan to have a mass-produced product such as embryonic/fetal/cloned stem cells that can be sold nationwide and have patentable intellectual property. Cloned stem cells derived from embryos with genetic defects represent the possibility of millions in patentable stem cell lines. Adult stem cell therapies are much better for people with diseases or injuries but generate an inferior business plan. In the case of adult stem cells where, in most cases, a person's own cells can be used, one can only develop a procedure that is generally not patentable according to new patent laws. However, the embryonic/fetal/cloned stem cells can lead to tremendous profits in the short run. Proof of this is the millions of dollars furnished by venture capitalists to help pass a measure that would provide $3 billion for stem cell research in California. . . .

There has been tremendous progress in adult stem cell research in the last few years. In . . . [one] study, adult stem cells transplanted into mice with liver injuries helped restore liver function within two to seven days. Transplantation of stem cells from adult human brain causes myelination to occur in a focally demyelinated spinal cord of the rat. Demyelination is common in spinal cord injury and disease states such as Multiple Sclerosis, and interferes with signal conduction between the neurons. Human cells from adult stem cells have been used to treat animal models of disease states. For example, human cells led to functional improvement in animal models of Parkinson's disease using human bone cells or neural stem cells. Human brain adult stem cells can even be obtained after death, so if a person's own stem cells are not used, there are other less objectionable alternatives. Another

98

alternative to the use of embryonic stem cells is human umbilical cord blood. Human umbilical cord blood has the potential to form neurons, as well as other cell types. Human umbilical cord blood injected intravenously caused a functional improvement when injected into experimental animals with traumatic brain injury or stroke. Bone marrow stromal cells from adult rats promote functional recovery after spinal cord injury in rats when given 1 week after injury, even when the cells are injected intravenously. Bone marrow stromal cells also will migrate to the site of a head injury when given intravenously and caused a functional improvement.

No Progress Shown Using Cloned Stem Cells

There has been progress in treating genetic disorders using adult stem cells or viruses in animal studies but no progress using cloned stem cells to treat genetic disorders in animals. In the case of genetic defects, there are several other alternatives to cloning. One is gene therapy that has been successfully used in mice and humans. More recently stem cells have been used as vehicles to deliver genes to the brain. Another valuable source of research into genetic disorders is adult stem cells that can be obtained from patients with genetic defects or a strong genetic predisposition to develop particular diseases.

Tremendous progress has been made using adult stem cells in clinical trials in treating diseases and injuries. . . .

Olfactory Mucosa

The olfactory mucosa lines the upper nasal cavity. The story begins with a brilliant neurologist from Portugal named Dr. Carlos Lima. He is also a pathologist that has published on the olfactory system and studied a collection of hundreds of olfactory mucosas from cadavers. In 1991 (the year before stem cells were first discovered in the brain), he decided to explore the potential of olfactory mucosa in the treatment of spinal cord injury because the olfactory system was the only system in the adult nervous system that regenerates. With very limited facilities, Dr. Lima began a study using fourteen guinea pigs in which the spinal cord was completely cut (transected). A week later, he implanted a piece of olfactory mucosa from the nose of that animal. He noticed that the guinea pigs that received the transplant were able to walk much better than the guinea pigs without the transplant. When he examined the spinal cords, the guinea pigs that improved showed tissue bridging between the two cut ends. We now know that there are several advantages to using the olfactory mucosa. The major advantage of the olfactory mucosa is its lifelong continual regenerative capacity, including the production of nerve cells. It is also accessible with minimally invasive techniques. The olfactory mucosa contains two cell types that we know help repair the nervous system: stem cells and olfactory ensheathing cells. The olfactory ensheathing cells encourage the growth of nerve cell processes (axons) and promote the myelination (covering on nerve cell processes that speed up the signal between neurons). Removal of part of the mucosa causes no permanent damage to olfaction (smelling). Problems of rejection, overgrowth, disease transmission, and ethical issues can be avoided because a person's own olfactory mucosa can be used. . . .

Clinical Trials by Dr. Carlos Lima and Colleagues in Portugal

Based on the animal results, Dr. Lima proposed a clinical trial in Portugal. . . . All of the people were treated in Portugal between six months and six years after their injury. The normal improvement, if any, that occurs after spinal cord injury takes place in the six months to a year after injury so these patients were treated at a time when no further improvements are expected. In this procedure, the area of the spinal cord damage is exposed surgically in patients with severe spinal cord injuries.

Then a small piece of olfactory mucosa in the upper part of the nose is removed from that same patient. The olfactory mucosa is then rinsed, cut in small pieces and placed in the spinal cord. . . .

It appeared that as in the animal studies, there was bridging of the injury. It is impossible to tell if there was tissue in a living individual but it is probable. All of the patients recovered well from the surgery. Olfaction returned to normal by three months after the surgery. All of the patients showed improvements. One of the patients regained bladder control at fifteen months after the surgery. Regaining bladder control is extremely important to patients with spinal cord injury. All but one of the patients gained feeling in some areas of their body where they previously had no feeling. All of the patients gained the ability to move certain muscles that they could not move before the olfactory mucosa treatment. . . .

A Remarkable Recovery

The surgery involved the removal of tissue from my olfactory sinus area and transplanting it into my spinal cord at the injury site. Both procedures, the harvesting of the tissue and the transplant were done at the same time. I was the tenth person in the world and the second American to have this procedure done.

After the surgery, I returned to California to continue physical therapy. I stayed there until July of 2003 and then returned back to San Antonio, Texas. At that time an MRI was taken and it revealed my spinal cord had begun to heal. Approximately 70% of the lesion now looked like normal spinal cord tissue.

I was also starting to regain feeling in my upper body and within six months I had regained feeling down to my abdomen. Improvements in my sensory feelings have continued until the present time. I can now feel down to my hip level and have started to regain feeling and some movement down to my legs.

Laura Dominguez, testimony before the U.S. Senate Committee on Commerce, Science, and Transportation, July 14, 2004.

In summary, all of Dr. Lima's patients that were treated with the olfactory mucosa showed some improvement. However, most of the patients did not have access to the best rehab facilities. This was very frustrating because it appeared that the patients would improve further if only better rehab facilities were available. In hopes of the patients being able to have access to better rehab facilities, several American patients that had requested the treatment were enrolled in the clinical trial. Some of these patients were carefully evaluated by physicians in the US before and after the olfactory mucosa treatment in Portugal. Two of these brave young women are here today to tell about their experiences.

Results in Two Americans After Olfactory Mucosa Treatment

Laura Dominguez had her accident on July 3, 2001. Afterwards she had no movement of her legs or hips and no feeling below her collarbone. Laura was 18 years old, tetraplegic with a lesion at the 6th cervical level that was 2 cm. long.

The lesion was mixed glial and connective tissue produced by a contusion and laceration. She went to a variety of excellent rehabilitation centers including Dr. John McDonald's in St. Louis and Project Walk in California. These centers helped her improve her upper body strength but she still could not move her hips, legs or feet and she had no feeling in these areas. In the U.S., Dr. Steve Hinderer and The Rehabilitation Institute of Michigan (currently headed by Dr. Jay Meythaler, associated with Detroit Medical Center and Wayne State University) began to look into the potential of Dr. Lima's procedures at the encouragement of Fred Nader whose daughter had a spinal cord injury. Almost two years after her accident, Laura and her family decided to go to Portugal to have the olfactory mucosa surgery performed by Dr. Lima and his team of doctors in March of last year [2003]. After her surgery, she regained some sensation and motor control of certain muscles. She is now able to point her toes. With braces, she is able to walk some distance. Although she has made remarkable improvements, a rehabilitation program that is actually tailored to these types of patients needs to be developed. Laura has received some help in developing a vigorous rehabilitation program from a talented karate instructor named Ivan Ujeta. Aquatherapy (water therapy) has proven to be particularly helpful. However, Laura and her family feel that rehabilitation programs need to be better developed.

Susan Fajt was in a car accident on Nov. 17, 2001. The spinal cord lesion was at thoracic level 7 and 8 and was about 3 cm. long. . . . She had no voluntary movement or sensory sensation below her level of injury. Susan had no sensory or motor activity on S4–S5 segments. About 2½ years after her injury, Susan went to Portugal to have the surgery performed by Dr. Lima and his team in June of last year (2003). She started to experience real gains around six months after the olfactory mucosa treatment with increased bladder control, sensory recovery and first movements of her thigh muscles. Susan and her father looked for the best rehab program; however, it seemed that the optimal rehabilitation program has yet to be designed. Her father John Fajt began, with Susan's help, to develop and patent devices such as a cross-trainer, standing wheel-chair (Venus craft), and camel wheel-chair (lowers or raises to facilitate going into and out of the pool) that would help her progress. She gained voluntary movements of her thigh muscles. In May [2004], at Dr. Albert Bohbot in France, Susan got more strength in these muscles and began walking on a walker with braces on her legs. . . .

The story of these two courageous young women dramatically shows the progress of adult stem cells and tissue and the need for further research into the less profitable, but more beneficial, direction of adult stem cells. Further work is needed to improve this technique, with the addition of other treatments including a rehabilitation program that will maximize the functional improvement.

"[Treatment using adult stem cells] produced an almost complete reversal of Parkinson's symptoms over four years."

Adult Stem Cell Treatments Are Curing Diseases

Richard M. Doerflinger

Richard M. Doerflinger is the deputy director of the Secretariat for Pro-Life Activities of the U.S. Conference of Catholic Bishops, and an adjunct fellow of bioethics and public policy at the National Catholic Bioethics Center. In the following viewpoint Doerflinger rejects the claim that embryonic stem cells derived from cloned embryos will provide useful treatments for diseases. He argues that Parkinson's disease and juvenile diabetes—the two diseases most often cited in the debate over embryonic stem cells—will not be helped by embryonic stem cells. Adult stem cells offer more promise, he contends, citing a case in which a Parkinson's patient was treated with his own adult stem cells and the illness almost completely disappeared.

As you read, consider the following questions:

1. Which countries have banned human cloning, according to Doerflinger?
2. According to the author, which country has produced a new stem cell line?
3. According to Ian Wilmut, as cited by Doerflinger, why is producing genetically matched stem cells through cloning unnecessary or useless for treating diseases?

R on Reagan's speech at the Democratic convention [on July 27, 2004] . . . was expected to urge expanded funding for stem cell research using so-called "spare" embryos—and to highlight these cells' potential for treating the Alzheimer's disease that took his father's life.

Ron Reagan's Radical Agenda

He did neither. He didn't even mention Alzheimer's, perhaps because even strong supporters of embryonic stem cell research say it is unlikely to be of use for that disease. (Reagan himself admitted this on a . . . segment of MSNBC's *Hardball*.) And he didn't talk about current debates on funding research using existing embryos. Instead he endorsed the more radical agenda of human cloning—mass-producing one's own identical twins in the laboratory so they can be exploited as (in his words) "your own personal biological repair kit" when disease or injury strikes.

Politically this was, to say the least, a gamble. Americans may be tempted to make use of embryos left over from fertility clinics, but most polls show them to be against human cloning for any purpose. Other advanced nations—Canada, Australia, France, Germany, Norway—have banned the practice completely. . . . Many groups and individuals who are "pro-choice" on abortion oppose research cloning, not least because it would require the mass exploitation of women to provide what Ron Reagan casually calls "donor eggs." And the potential "therapeutic" benefits of cloning are even more speculative than those of embryonic stem cell research—the worldwide effort even to obtain viable stem cells from cloned embryos has already killed hundreds of embryos and produced exactly one stem cell line, in South Korea.

What Is Really at Stake

But precisely for these reasons, Ron Reagan should be praised for his candor. The scientists and patient groups promoting embryonic stem cell research know that the current debate on funding is a mere transitional step. For years they have supported the mass manufacture of human embryos through cloning, as the logical and necessary goal of their agenda, but lately they have been coy about this as they fight for the more popular slogan of "stem cell research." With his speech Reagan has removed the mask, and allowed us to debate what is really at stake.

He claimed in his speech, of course, that what is at stake in this debate is the lives of millions of patients with devastating diseases. But by highlighting Parkinson's disease and juvenile diabetes as two diseases most clearly justifying the move to human cloning, he failed to do his homework. These are two of the diseases that pro-cloning scientists now admit will probably *not* be helped by research cloning.

Amazing Progress with Adult Stem Cells

Scientists have made amazing progress in using stem cells and other avenues to cure debilitating diseases. But none of the advances now in human clinical trials come from destroying embryos. They come from the morally acceptable avenues that much of the scientific establishment has dismissed as inadequate.

Richard M. Doerflinger, *National Right to Life News*, December 2002.

Scottish cloning expert Ian Wilmut, for example, wrote in the *British Medical Journal* in February [2004] that producing genetically matched stem cells through cloning is probably quite unnecessary for treating any neurological disease. Recent findings suggest that the nervous system is "immune privileged," and will not generally reject stem cells from a human who is genetically different. He added that cloning is probably useless for auto-immune diseases like juvenile diabetes, where the body mistakenly rejects its own insulin-producing cells as though they were foreign. "In such cases," he wrote, "transfer of immunologically identical cells to a patient is expected to induce the same rejection."

Wilmut's observations cut the ground out from under Ron Reagan's simple-minded claim that cloning is needed to avoid tissue rejection. For some diseases, genetically matched cells are unnecessary; for others, they are useless, because they only replicate the genetic profile that is part of the problem. (Ironically, for Alzheimer's both may be true—cloning may be unnecessary to avoid tissue rejection in the brain, and useless because the cloned cells would have the same genetic defect that may lead to Alzheimer's.) Reagan declared that this debate requires us to "choose between . . . reason and ignorance," but he did not realize which side has the monopoly on ignorance.

A Cure for Parkinson's Is Already Here

That ignorance poses an obstacle to real advances that are right before our eyes. Two weeks before Ron Reagan declared that a treatment for Parkinson's may arrive "ten or so years from now," using "the material of our own bodies," a Parkinson's patient and his doctor quietly appeared before Congress to point out that this has already been done. Dennis Turner was treated in 1999 by Dr. Michel Levesque of Cedars-Sinai Medical Center in Los Angeles, using his own adult neural stem cells. Dr. Levesque did not use the Rube Goldberg method of trying to turn those cells into a cloned embryo and then killing the embryo to get stem cells—he just grew Turner's own adult stem cells in the lab, and turned them directly into dopamine-producing cells. And with just one injection, on one side of Turner's brain, he produced an almost complete reversal of Parkinson's symptoms over four years.

Turner stopped shaking, could eat without difficulty, could put in his own contact lenses again, and resumed his avocation of big-game photography—on one occasion scrambling up a tree in Africa to escape a charging rhinoceros.

Amazingly, while this advance has been presented at national and international scientific conferences and featured on ABC-TV in Chicago, the scientific establishment supporting embryonic stem cell research has almost completely ignored it, and most news media have obediently imposed a virtual news blackout on it. That did not change even after the results were presented to the Senate Commerce Subcommittee on Science, Technology and Space . . . [in July 2004]. Pro-cloning Senators on the panel actually seemed angry at the witnesses, for trying to distract them from their fixation on destroying embryos.

Turner also testified that his symptoms have begun to return, especially arising from the side of his brain that was left untreated, and he would like to get a second treatment. For that he will have to wait. Dr. Levesque has received insufficient appreciation and funding for his technique, and is still trying to put together the funds for broader clinical trials—as most Parkinson's foundations and NIH [National Institutes of Health] peer reviewers look into the starry distance of Ron Reagan's dreams about embryonic stem cells.

But hey, who cares about real Parkinson's patients when there's a Brave New World to sell?

> *"Scientists cannot obtain pluripotent cells without destroying the four-day-old embryos from which they come."*

Embryonic Stem Cell Research Destroys Human Life

Jacqueline Lee

Many people oppose embryonic stem cell research because embryos must be destroyed in the process. They consider this practice to be ethically wrong—whether the embryo is the result of cloning or fertility treatments. Jacqueline Lee is a freelance writer living in Arizona. In the following viewpoint, she describes the death of her mother from a rare disease in which the body's immune system turns on itself. Lee maintains that she would have done anything to save her mother—anything except use embryonic stem cell therapy. While stem cell research has brought encouraging results in treating this disease, Lee asserts she cannot support embryonic stem cell research because it involves destroying nascent human life in order to extract the stem cells. Adult stem cell therapy does not kill embryos and also shows promise in treating diseases. Lee concludes that the goal of curing diseases does not justify destroying embryos.

As you read, consider the following questions:

1. Which stem cell research—embryonic or adult—receives more investment capital for research, according to Scott Gottlieb, as cited by the author?
2. What percentage of Catholics support stem cell research, according to Lee?

Jacqueline Lee, "Embryonic Stem Cells: The End Doesn't Justify the Means," *U.S. Catholic*, vol. 67, January 2002, p. 24. Copyright © 2002 by Claretian Publications. Reproduced by permission of *U.S. Catholic* magazine, www.uscatholic.org.

Watching someone you love turn to stone before your eyes can definitely affect your perspective on the embryonic stem-cell research debate. In 1999, my mother was diagnosed with scleroderma, which literally means hard skin. For a person with this rare disease, the immune system, which is supposed to attack the pathogens that make us ill, turns instead on healthy body tissues. Symptoms may begin with tightening and thickening of the skin along with joint and muscle pain. Patients may then develop Raynaud's phenomenon, a condition in which the body's extremities change color in response to temperature. Others may develop calcinosis, white lumps beneath the skin that can erupt, leaving painful ulcers.

My mother's first symptom was shortness of breath. The disease viciously attacked her lungs and other internal organs, and she died of respiratory failure within seven months of her diagnosis. During that time, she lost the ability to get up from a sitting position without assistance. She lost 50 pounds because she could not eat anything without vomiting. She lost her ability to breathe. In the end, instead of praying for her recovery, I began to pray that she would be released from her struggle with the disease. As soon as she died, I begged God for the chance to take that prayer back.

The Body's "Master Cells"

According to research presented [in 2001] . . . by University of Florida professor of medicine John R. Wingard, stem-cell transplants show remarkable promise in treating not only scleroderma but also other autoimmune diseases like multiple sclerosis and lupus. Essentially, stem cells are the body's "master cells." They can differentiate into other types of cells, from brain cells to skin cells. Feasibly, stem cells might be injected into the nervous system to replace tissues damaged by strokes, Alzheimer's, Parkinson's, or spinal cord injuries.

I am excited about the potential of stem-cell therapies, but recent demands that the federal government fund research on embryonic stem cells frighten me. Extracting stem cells from embryos proves contentious, of course, because embryos must be destroyed in order to obtain the cells.

Supporters of embryonic stem-cell research cite two main

advantages of embryonic stem cells—both of them, ultimately, economic. According to the National Institutes of Health, stem cells from embryos, so-called "pluripotent" cells, are more flexible than adult stem cells and can thus be manipulated into more types of body tissues, including bone, skin, and muscle. Those who support federal funding of embryonic stem-cell research claim that pluripotent cells are more useful than adult stem cells because they possess these remarkable powers of transformation. In addition, scientists can generate an unlimited number of embryonic stem cells in the laboratory. Because adult cells are more difficult to obtain, embryos would be a more cost-effective source of cells.

"We are now witnessing the gradual restructuring of American culture according to ideals of utility, productivity, and cost-effectiveness," wrote the U.S. Catholic bishops in *Living the Gospel of Life: A Challenge to American Catholics.* "It is a culture where moral questions are submerged by a river of goods and services."

But opponents of embryonic research, ironically, are able to cite the economic argument, too. According to a recent article by Scott Gottlieb in the *American Spectator*, investors of venture capital currently fund adult stem-cell research much more frequently than they fund embryonic research. Why? Embryonic cells have never been used in humans, but adult cells have.

Opponents also note that embryonic cells can, at times, be too flexible. Gottlieb notes that the injection of pluripotent cells in mice, for instance, has caused the growth of tumors consisting of numerous body tissue types; the cells did not integrate themselves into damaged tissues as scientists hoped they would. Also, conceivably, a transplanted embryonic stem cell could be rejected by the recipient's body—much like the body tries to reject a transplanted organ. Adult stem cells, however, are more specialized and, because adult stem cells are harvested from the patient's own body, rejection is not a factor.

Apart from medical and economic arguments, we as Catholics must wade through the ambiguous moral arguments both for and against embryonic research. While many prolife Catholic organizations, including the National Catholic Bioethics Center, have staunchly opposed stem-cell research, according to a *Wall Street Journal*/NBC News Poll, a majority of Catholics surveyed—72 percent—support it.

Sen. Orrin Hatch of Utah, a leading supporter of embryonic research, argues that "a frozen embryo in a refrigerator in a clinic" is not the same as "a fetus developing in a mother's womb." These frozen embryos, his supporters say, have the potential to develop into life—but the embryos themselves are not technically alive.

Human Embryos Are Human Beings

No one believes that stem cells—embryonic or otherwise—are human beings. Those of us who oppose embryonic-stem-cell harvesting object to the practice because it necessarily involves the killing of human embryos. And human embryos are nothing other than human beings in the embryonic stage of their natural development. . . .

Just as each of us was once an adolescent, and before that a child, and before that an infant, and before that a fetus, each of us was once an embryo. (By contrast, none of us was ever a somatic cell, or an ovum, or sperm cell.) The human "adolescent," "infant," "fetus," and "embryo" are not different kinds of entities (or, as philosophers say, "different substances"); these terms refer to *stages* in the natural development of a human being.

Robert P. George, "Snake Oil," *National Review Online*, July 28, 2004.

Many bioethicists, however, dismiss that argument as pointless rationalization. If all humans begin as embryos, how can embryos not be considered "alive"? Furthermore, if these embryos are alive, then extracting embryonic stem cells violates at least three principles of the Nuremberg Code, which lays out principles scientists must observe when conducting research on human subjects. First, scientists must always obtain the voluntary consent of every human research subject. Embryos, of course, cannot give their consent. Also, when scientists create embryos specifically for the purposes of experimentation, the embryos do not even have parents who can speak on their behalf.

Second, the Nuremberg Code states that human subjects should be protected "against even remote possibilities of injury, disability, or death." Third, the Nuremberg Code requires that experiments on human subjects must yield results "unprocurable by any other means of study."

No Need for Embryonic Cell Research

If experimental treatments involving adult cells have already furnished promising results, why do we need embryonic cells? And if embryonic research violates the codes we have established to protect human dignity, how can we, as moral people, even consider carrying it out?

As Tommy Thompson, [former] U.S. Secretary of Health and Human Services—and a prominent Catholic—observes, "There is nothing easy about this issue. It balances our respect for human life with our highest hopes for alleviating human suffering." True, pluripotent cells in and of themselves cannot develop into human beings. However, scientists cannot obtain pluripotent cells without destroying the four-day-old embryos from which they come. "As long as embryos are destroyed as part of the research enterprise," says the National Bioethics Advisory Council, "researchers using embryonic stem cells (and those who fund them) will be complicit in the death of embryos."

With his decision in August [2001], President [George W.] Bush has already authorized limited funding for research on existing stem-cell lines. . . . Although many respect Bush's compromise, my own fear is that his willingness to allow a little funding has paved the way for steady relaxation of current restrictions.

The Ends Do Not Justify the Means

Ultimately, it comes down to this: can we really justify the willful destruction of human embryos by arguing that "the end justifies the means"? Is it acceptable to undermine the dignity of human life in the name of medical progress?

Perhaps many of us are looking at this issue through swollen eyes blurred by tears. We have all seen the suffering brought on by degenerative illness, either in ourselves or in someone we love. Our hearts ache for those who suffer, and we want to do anything by any means to stop it.

But, no matter how laudable that aim may be, it cannot

justify the destruction of a developing human life. In the words of Charlotte Bronte's Jane Eyre, "Law and principles are not for times when there is no temptation: They are for such moments as this, when body and soul rise in mutiny against their rigor. If at my individual convenience I might break them, what would be their worth?"

My heart ached for my mother, and today it aches for all those who suffer from disease and injury; but, no matter how deep my desire to ease that suffering may be, it cannot justify the destruction of a developing human life. I wish that my mother had been strong enough to undergo a stem-cell transplant. I would have done anything to save her.

Well, almost anything. I would not have been complicit in the destruction of human life, even if the destruction of that life could have saved hers. To me, a praiseworthy end could never have justified such a destructive means.

"The assertion that a single fertilized cell is a 'human being' . . . require[s] challenge on conservative grounds, as [it has] never been approved by American law or accepted as common convention."

Embryonic Stem Cell Research Does Not Destroy Human Life

Jeffrey Hart

Opposition to embryonic stem cell research often centers on the argument that embryos—whether the result of cloning or in vitro fertilization—are human beings. In the following viewpoint, Jeffrey Hart, an editor with *National Review*, rejects this argument. Specifically, he criticizes *National Review* for its editorials that condemn embryonic stem cell research on the premise that embryos are human beings. According to Hart, embryos have the potential to become human, but they are not yet human. Nor does any American law recognize the embryo as a human being. Because the embryos are not human beings, Hart concludes harvesting embryos' stem cells in an attempt to cure diseases is morally justifiable.

As you read, consider the following questions:

1. According to Hart, why does the destruction of fertilized cells produced for in vitro fertilization provoke no public outcry?
2. How does Hart describe the embryos used for stem-cell research?
3. Which universities are pursuing stem-cell research, according to the author?

Jeffrey Hart, "NR on Stem Cells," *National Review*, vol. 56, April 19, 2004, p. 24. Copyright © 2004 by the National Review, Inc., 215 Lexington Ave., New York, NY 10016. Reproduced by permission.

National Review has consistently taken a position on stem-cell research that requires some discussion here. Three editorials early [in 2004] were based on the assertion that a single fertilized cell is a "human being." This premise—and the conclusions drawn from it—require challenge on conservative grounds, as they have never been approved by American law or accepted as common convention.

Grating Demands

The first 2004 editorial appeared in the January 26 issue, and made a series of assertions about recent legislation in New Jersey. It included the notion that it is now "possible" to create a human embryo there—through cloning—that, at age eight months, could be sold for research. But this dystopian fantasy could become fact in no American jurisdiction.

In the March 8 *NR* [*National Review*] we read another editorial; this one achieved greater seriousness. Still, it called for a "new law" that "would say that human beings, however small and young, may not be treated instrumentally and may not be deliberately destroyed."

In all of the editorials, we are asked to accept the insistent dogma that a single fertilized cell is a "human being, however small and young," and is not to be "deliberately destroyed."

This demand grates—because such "human beings" are deliberately destroyed all the time, and such "mass homicide" arouses no public outcry. In fact, there are about 100,000 fertilized cells now frozen in maternity clinics. These are the inevitable, and so deliberate, by-products of in vitro fertilization, accepted by women who cannot conceive children naturally. No wonder there has been no outcry: Where reality shows medical waste that would otherwise lie useless, *NR's* characterization of these frozen embryos as "small and young" makes one think of the Gerber baby.

A False Assertion

The entire *NR* case against stem-cell research rests, like a great inverted pyramid, on the single assertion that these cells are "human beings"—a claim that is not self-evidently true. Even when the naked eye is aided by a microscope, these cells—"zygotes," to use the proper terminology—do not look like human beings. That resemblance does not emerge even as the zygote grows into the hundred-cell organism, about the size of a pinhead, called a "blastocyst." This is the level of development at which stem cells are produced: The researcher is not interested in larger embryos, much less full-blown, for-sale fetuses.

I myself have never met anyone who bites into an apple, gazes upon the seeds there, and sees a grove of apple trees. I think we must conclude, if we are to use language precisely, that the single fertilized cell is a developing or potential human being—many of which are destroyed during in vitro fertilization, and even in the course of natural fertilization. But just as a seed—a potential apple tree—is no orchard, a potential child is not yet a human being.

Idea Versus Actuality

There is more to this matter than biology: In question is *NR*'s very theory of—and approach to—politics. Classic and valuable arguments in this magazine have often taken the form of Idea (or paradigm) versus Actuality. Here are a few such debates that have shaped the magazine, a point of interest especially to new readers.

Very early in *NR*'s history, the demand for indisputably conservative candidates gave way to William F. Buckley Jr.'s decisive formulation that *NR* should prefer "the most conservative electable candidate." WFB thus corrected his refusal to vote for. [Dwight D.] Eisenhower, who was at least more conservative than [Adlai] Stevenson. Senior editor James Burnham, a realist, also voted for Ike; in his decision, Actuality won out.

In the 1956 crisis in Hungary, Burnham's profoundly held Idea about the necessity for Liberation in Europe contrasted with Eisenhower's refusal, based on Actuality, to intervene in a landlocked nation where Soviet ground and air superiority was decisive. But later on, Burnham, choosing Actuality over the Idea, saw much sooner than most conservatives that [Richard] Nixon's containment and "Vietnamization" could not work in South Vietnam, which was a sieve. The "peace" that was "at hand" in 1972 was the peace of the grave.

A final example: In the late 1960s, senior editor Brent

Bozell's theoretical demand for perfect Catholic morality—argued in a very fine exchange with another senior editor, Frank Meyer—was rejected by *NR*.

In Vitro Fertilization

Thus the tension between Idea and Actuality has a long tradition at *NR*, revived by this question of stem cells. Ultimately, American constitutional decision-making rests upon the "deliberate consent" of a self-governing people. Such decisionmaking by consensus usually accords no participant everything he desires, and thus is non-utopian. Just try an absolute, ideological ban on in vitro fertilization, for example, and observe the public response.

Americans Support Therapeutic Cloning Research to Produce Stem Cells

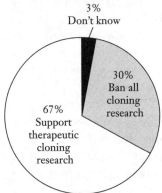

Coalition for the Advancement of Medical Research, "New Poll Shows More than Two Thirds of Americans Support Therapeutic Cloning Research to Produce Stem Cells," March 19, 2003.

In fact, an editorial (*NR*, August 6, 2001) has held that even in vitro fertilization is hard to justify morally. Understandably, *NR* has soft-pedaled this opinion: The magazine's view that a single cell is a "human being" has never been expressed in or embraced by American law. It represents an absolutization of the "human being" claim for a single cell. It stands in contradiction to the "deliberate sense" theory *NR* has heretofore espoused. And, at this very moment, it is being contradicted in the Actual world of research practice.

Recently, for instance, a Harvard researcher produced 17 stem-cell "lines" from the aforementioned leftover frozen cells. The researcher's goal is not homicide, of course, but the possible cure of dreadful diseases. It seems to me that the prospect of eliminating horrible, disabling ailments justifies, morally, using cells that are otherwise doomed. Morality requires the weighing of results, and the claim to a "right to life" applies in both directions. Those lifting that phrase from the Declaration of Independence do not often add "liberty and the pursuit of happiness," there given equal standing as "rights"—rights that might be more widely enjoyed in the wake of stem-cell advances.

An Unsustainable Position

As I said earlier, the evolution of *NR* as a magazine that matters has involved continuing arguments between Idea and Actuality. Here, the Idea that a single fertilized cell is a human being, and that destroying one is a homicide, is not sustainable. That is the basis—the only basis—for NR's position thus far on stem-cell research. Therefore NR's position on the whole issue is unsustainable.

Buckley has defined conservatism as the "politics of reality." That is the strength of conservatism, a Burkean[1] strength, and an anti-utopian one. I have never heard a single cytologist affirming the proposition that a single cell is a "human being"; here, Actuality will prevail, as usual.

Universities Pursue Stem-Cell Research

In recommending against federal funding for most stem-cell research, President George W. Bush stated that 60 lines of stem cells that already exist are adequate for current research. The National Institutes of Health has said that this is incorrect. There are in fact 15 lines, and these are not adequate even for current research. The president was misinformed. But Actuality is gaining ground nonetheless: Harvard University has recently announced the formation of a $100 million Harvard Stem Cell Institute. And Harvard

1. A reference to eighteenth-century British statesman, Edmund Burke.

physicians are conducting community-education programs to counter misinformation (Reuters, March 3). "Scientists at Harvard University announced . . . that they had created 17 batches of stem cells from human embryos in defiance of efforts by President Bush to limit such research. 'What we have done is to make use of previously frozen human fertilized eggs that otherwise were going to be discarded,' [Dr. Douglas] Melton told reporters in a telephone briefing."

Not unexpectedly, and after losing one of its top scientists in the field to Cambridge (England), the University of California, Berkeley, announced that it was pursuing stem-cell research. Other UCs also made such announcements, and California state funding has been promised. It is easy to see that major research universities across the nation—and in any nation that can afford them—will either follow or lose their top scientists in this field. Experience shows that it is folly to reject medical investigation, a folly the universities and private-sector researchers will be sure to avoid.

Weak in theory, and irrelevant in practice, opposition to stem-cell research is now an irrelevance across the board; on this matter, even the president has made himself irrelevant. All this was to be expected: The only surprise has been the speed with which American research is going forward. It is pleasant to have the private sector intervene, as at Harvard, not to mention the initiatives of the states. In practical terms, this argument is over *National Review* should not make itself irrelevant by trying to continue it.

Periodical Bibliography

The following articles have been selected to supplement the diverse views presented in this chapter.

Janet L. Dolgin — "Embryonic Discourse: Abortion, Stem Cells and Cloning," *Issues in Law & Medicine*, April 2004.

William FitzPatrick — "Surplus Embryos, Nonreproductive Cloning, and the Intend/Foresee Distinction," *Hastings Center Report*, May/June 2003.

Amy Laura Hall — "Price to Pay: The Misuse of Embryos," *Christian Century*, June 1, 2004.

David Hess — "Therapeutic Cloning Ignores Fate of Embryos," *Atlanta Journal-Constitution*, May 1, 2002.

Erika Jonietz — "Cloning, Stem Cells, and Medicine's Future," *Technology Review*, June 2003.

Jonathan Knight — "Biologists Fear Cloning Hype Will Undermine Stem-Cell Research," *Nature*, August 19, 2004.

Don Marquis — "Stem Cell Research: The Failure of Bioethics," *Free Inquiry*, Winter 2002.

Ramesh Ponnuru — "The Magazine Is Right," *National Review*, April 19, 2004.

Seattle Times — "Time for Rational Stem-Cell Research," January 26, 2005.

Wesley J. Smith — "The C-Word," *National Review Online*, July 28, 2004.

M. Spriggs — "Therapeutic Cloning Research and Ethical Oversight," *Journal of Medical Ethics*, August 2003.

Joni Eareckson Tada — "The Threat of Biotech," *Christianity Today*, March 2003.

CHAPTER 4

Should Cloning Be Banned?

Chapter Preface

After the announcement in 1997 that researchers in Scotland had cloned a sheep from an adult cell, the world was suddenly forced to confront the issue of cloning. Nearly every nation agrees that reproductive human cloning—cloning a person with the intent of producing a human baby—should be banned. More than 150 of the almost 200 nations in the world have banned this research. However, not every country believes that therapeutic cloning research—cloning a human cell in order to study or treat diseases—should be banned. Some countries have embraced the possibilities offered by cloning technology; these governments and researchers see promising advances in cloning technology for treating several debilitating and incurable diseases. This disagreement over which cloning practices should be banned has led to deep divisions among the world's governments.

In 1997 in the United States, the President's National Bioethics Advisory Commission recommended a moratorium on human cloning. According to the commission, "Any attempt to clone human beings via somatic cell nuclear transfer techniques is uncertain in its prospects, is unacceptably dangerous to the fetus and therefore, morally unacceptable." The U.S. Congress has tried several times in the late 1990s and early 2000s to ban all forms of human cloning, but its efforts have not been successful due to the divisions among its members over the value and possibilities offered by therapeutic cloning.

Worried that researchers may try to escape a nationwide ban on cloning by doing their work in another country where human cloning research is legal—or where scientific work is not closely monitored—the United States has also tried, with support from several other countries, to persuade the United Nations to ban all forms of human cloning. While the UN has been unable to reach a consensus on a global treaty that would have banned all forms of human cloning research, it did pass a nonbinding declaration in the spring of 2005 urging member nations to prohibit all research.

Of the thirty-four countries that voted against the declaration, many did so, they said, because it made no distinction between cloning for human reproductive purpose—which they oppose—and cloning for therapeutic purposes—which they support. Some of the countries opposed to the declaration—for example, Britain, Korea, and China—already have laboratories in place where their scientists are working on therapeutic cloning research; consequently, their scientists would not be required to abide by the UN's declaration. Britain's UN ambassador, Jones Parry, explains why his country will not change its position on therapeutic cloning. It has, he said, the "potential to revolutionize medicine in this century in the way that antibiotics did in the last" century.

Despite the almost worldwide aversion to cloning human babies, several researchers have, in recent years, announced that they have cloned human children. No baby has been produced to prove the claims, however, and most scientists have discounted the announcements as hoaxes. But Ian Wilmut, the embryologist behind the cloning of Dolly, believes it is only a matter of time before a cloned baby is born, whether or not there is a worldwide ban on the procedure. In fact, his cloning research may even result in a cloned baby sooner than expected; Wilmut announced in early 2005 that he intended to start cloning human embryos for therapeutic cloning research.

Even though most governments have banned human cloning and much of the world is against cloning to produce children, there will always be scientists who will continue their research into trying to be the first to clone a human being. The authors in the following chapter discuss whether banning cloning is an effective means of controlling the research.

> *"A ban on human cloning for both research and reproductive purposes would be the most effective and ethically responsible safeguard against the birth of human beings via cloning."*

All Cloning Research Should Be Banned

William P. Cheshire Jr. et al.

In the following viewpoint William P. Cheshire Jr. and his associates contend that the only way to protect against the birth of cloned human babies is to ban all forms of human cloning, both reproductive and therapeutic. They argue that if therapeutic cloning is permitted, it is only a short step to cloning a human baby. Furthermore, the first rule of medicine is to do no harm to the patient, and both reproductive and therapeutic cloning violate this rule. Reproductive cloning has an extremely high rate of death and deformity, and therapeutic cloning kills the embryo. Therefore, the authors contend, all forms of human cloning must be opposed. The authors are affiliated with the Center for Bioethics and Human Dignity, the Center for Clinical Bioethics at Georgetown University, and the C. Everett Koop Institute at Dartmouth College.

As you read, consider the following questions:
1. In the authors' opinion, why would a partial ban on human cloning be unenforceable?
2. In the authors' opinion, why does human cloning fail to qualify as a healing act?

William P. Cheshire Jr. et al., "Stem Cell Research: Why Medicine Should Reject Human Cloning," *Mayo Clinic Proceedings*, vol. 78, August 2003, pp. 1,010–14, 1,016–17. Copyright © 2003 by the Mayo Foundation. Reproduced by permission of MFMER.

S peculation that the world's first human clone may have been born, combined with reports that human embryos have been cloned for research purposes, calls for careful public and professional scrutiny of the critically important matter of human cloning.

Human cloning is the asexual production of a human being whose genetic makeup is nearly identical to that of a currently or previously existing individual. Whereas the deliberations of international, national, and state regulatory bodies have, in most cases, favored the prohibition of what has been called *reproductive* cloning—in which a cloned human embryo is created with the intent that a human clone will be born—they have differed considerably over what has been termed *research* cloning. Research cloning involves the creation of a cloned human embryo for the purpose of scientific investigation of early human development or for medical research aimed at developing treatments for disease. Because embryonic stem cells are pluripotent, having the capacity to differentiate into the full range of human tissues, some believe that these cells hold the potential to revolutionize medicine by providing a source of replacement tissue that might one day restore the health of persons suffering from a variety of debilitating conditions. Transplanted embryonic stem cells derived from a patient's clone may be compatible (as would adult-derived stem cells from the patient) with that patients immune system and hence, in principle, be resistant to immune rejection.

Our contention is that human cloning should not be permitted, whether for research or reproductive purposes. While we enthusiastically affirm the importance of medical research and ardently support the goal of healing people, we believe that the harms human cloning would bring to medicine would exceed the anticipated benefits.

Reproductive Cloning

An overwhelming majority of scientists, health care professionals, policy makers, bioethicists, theologians, and the general public have indicated their opposition to the birth of cloned human beings. The following concerns have been advanced.

Human cloning would be hazardous to the gestating clone and the surrogate mother. The current state of nonhuman animal cloning technology is so rudimentary that the procedure has resulted in a staggeringly high occurrence of severe physical and genetic defects and premature aging in cloned offspring. Embryologists estimate that a single successful human cloning might come at the cost of hundreds of failed attempts. Even if issues of safety were overcome, which is unlikely apart from unethical human experimentation, compelling ethical objections remain.

Human cloning would signify an egregious disrespect for personal autonomy. In forcing on the human clone a selected identity bound to certain, perhaps unfulfilled, expectations placed on the genetic original, cloning would frame that person's life and limit that person's autonomy permanently. Cloning would also encumber that person with profound emotional burdens. The cloned individual would not be born with the special privilege of having a unique genetic identity, but rather would always live in the shadow of the other person whom he or she was intended to duplicate genetically. The social stigma of being known as a clone, combined with confused parentage and expectations of measuring up to the achievements of the genetic original or of "replacing" a deceased loved one, could result in unimaginable psychological turmoil. If cloning became common practice, its deviation from the traditional design and accompanying moral responsibilities of the human family might well disrupt social stability.

Moreover, cloning brings to mind images of assembly-line manufacture more suited for the making of replaceable appliances than unique human beings. Deeply held public intuition thus regards the prospect of human cloning to be a repugnant departing, from the intimate and richly meaningful process of natural procreation. Unlike other reproductive technologies that assist procreation, cloning seeks to produce a human being with a particular genetic code. It is not technology that we oppose, but rather the misuse of technology that enables some people to exert nearly absolute control over the genetic makeup of others. This substitution of human genetic replication for procreation would constitute a serious affront to human dignity. If cloning proceeds along its current path of development, it will foster a grave devaluation of humanity. Whether cloning were to become a widespread or an occasional practice, its acceptance would shift societal attitudes away from appreciating people as distinct individuals and toward a new way of sizing up people as useful or attractive commodities of technology assembled to satisfy others' expectations.

All Human Cloning Is Wrong

I believe all human cloning is wrong, and both forms of cloning ought to be banned, for the following reasons. First, anything other than a total ban on human cloning would be unethical. Research cloning would contradict the most fundamental principle of medical ethics, that no human life should be exploited or extinguished for the benefit of another.

Yet a law permitting research cloning, while forbidding the birth of a cloned child, would require the destruction of nascent human life. Secondly, anything other than a total ban on human cloning would be virtually impossible to enforce. Cloned human embryos created for research would be widely available in laboratories and embryo farms. Once cloned embryos were available, implantation would take place. Even the tightest regulations and strict policing would not prevent or detect the birth of cloned babies.

Third, the benefits of research cloning are highly speculative. Advocates of research cloning argue that stem cells obtained from cloned embryos would be injected into a genetically identical individual without risk of tissue rejection. But there is evidence, based on animal studies, that cells derived from cloned embryos may indeed be rejected.

George W. Bush, remarks by the President on Human Cloning Legislation, April 10, 2002.

Some will defend human cloning as a right of reproductive liberty that ought never be restricted. However, there exists no inalienable right to engage in human cloning as a means of realizing one's desire for a child, regardless of the particular motivation behind such a desire. Furthermore, although reproduction is a private matter, development and implementation of genetic technology on which reproductive decisions will be based are matters of definite public interest. No reason has been advanced that is weighty enough to justify overlooking the considerable hazards described herein and resorting to cloning as a means of human reproduction. The disturbing dangers of human cloning to public health and well-being should be of concern to physicians in particular because the menacing key to this Pandora's box is a medical procedure.

Implications of a Partial Ban

Proposals to ban human cloning for purposes of reproduction have attracted broad support. However, enacting a ban solely on reproductive cloning, while simultaneously permitting research cloning, would almost certainly fail to achieve its stated objective. For the following reasons, we contend that a partial ban could well result in instances of both types of cloning, leading to a society that most Americans would deem undesirable.

Unenforceability

First, a partial ban would be unenforceable. If a ban on reproductive cloning only were adopted, enforcement would necessarily entail the legally mandated destruction of human embryos created for research cloning. Such required destruction would not only constitute a form of clear discrimination against a class of human beings based on the means of conception but also would likely be objected to or wholly disregarded by many, particularly by those who desire to implant the embryos. Because the legality of terminating the lives of unborn human beings by abortion is frequently defended as a matter of personal choice, it is difficult to imagine that most Americans would welcome a governmental policy that mandated the destruction of embryonic human life and the punishment of those who defied the law (either by knowingly implanting a cloned human embryo or by giving birth to a human clone). Such acts of defiance would be viewed by many as the private exercise of a reproductive option entitled to certain protections, effectively circumventing a partial ban. Although we do not believe that people have a right (rooted in reproductive liberty) to *create* human beings via cloning, we nevertheless maintain that parents should never be forced to destroy their offspring, *once created*, regardless of their method of origin.

Currently, the parents of embryos created via in vitro fertilization (IVF), for example, are given a great measure of decision-making power regarding the fate of their embryos. Some fertility clinics exceed clinical policy requirements in their efforts to determine parents' wishes regarding stored embryos, and all clinics are obligated to honor decisions both for and against implantation. Our autonomy-steeped culture would surely have difficulty accepting a policy that would deny people the same choice simply because their embryos were created through cloning.

Regardless of their legality, both IVF and reproductive cloning are technologies that lie within the realm of reproduction. Because of the private context of reproduction and the underregulation of the US fertility industry, prohibiting the implantation of cloned human embryos would be a formidable task met with considerable resistance, regardless of whether reproductive cloning is legally permissible. Of importance, although public consensus favors a law prohibiting the reproductive cloning of human beings, continued legislative stalemate on proposals to adopt a comprehensive cloning ban prohibiting both research and reproductive cloning might mean that even reproductive cloning would remain legal.

If cloned human embryos were created in the laboratory for research purposes only, the mandate that they not be implanted or otherwise allowed to progress toward birth would prove extremely difficult to uphold. Therefore, the birth of cloned human beings—the very thing that a ban on reproductive cloning should prevent—would likely result.

Compassionate Transgressions

Second, if cloned human embryos were available for research, appeals to compassion within the privacy of the physician-patient relationship would likely lead to their implantation. Consider the following hypothetical scenarios.

A cloned human embryo is created with the intent of producing tissue needed to save the life of a seriously ill child. Before the tissue can be obtained, the ill child dies. Her grieving parents, distraught over their tragic loss, request that the embryo be implanted so that they may have another child who is a near genetic duplicate of the daughter whom they so desperately miss.

A man agrees to be cloned with the intent of donating the resultant embryo to research. Subsequent to creation of the cloned embryo, he learns that both he and his wife are infertile. Realizing that their prospect for having a genetically related child suddenly appears to be compromised, the man changes his mind and requests that his clone be implanted in his wife instead of donated to research.

In such cases, it would be difficult for many physicians to deny the wishes of those desiring to implant a cloned embryo.

Ineffective Detection

Third, violations of a partial ban would often go unnoticed. If laboratory creation of cloned human embryos was permitted but implantation of such embryos was banned, it would be infeasible to monitor the fate of each and every cloned embryo. The somatic cell nuclear transfer procedure typically results in the creation of multiple embryos. To prevent a single embryo from being implanted within the private context of the physician-patient relationship would surely prove to be impossible. Moreover, policies that would require genetic testing of every neonate at birth to ensure that he or she is not a clone (and that would penalize the parties responsible for implanting a cloned embryo) would likely be regarded as a violation of privacy. Even if such testing were allowed, it would fail to ensure that reproductive cloning had not occurred because the baby could be a clone of an unknown or unrevealed person, rather than being a near genetic duplicate of one of the parents.

As a result, threats to levy fines or inflict other punishments would not always deter those wishing to engage in technology they perceived to be undetectable. Policies that prohibit, and penalize those who request or assist in, the implantation of cloned human embryos would therefore ultimately fail to prevent reproductive cloning once cloned human embryos were produced for research purposes. . . .

A More Effective Policy

A ban on human cloning for both research and reproductive purposes would be the most effective and ethically responsible safeguard against the birth of human beings via cloning.

Once human embryos were developed to the stage at which stem cells are present, a primary objective of research cloning, they would also be suitable for implantation. Then, as we have illustrated, the birth of cloned human embryos would be only a short step away; once a cloned human embryo was implanted in a woman's body, no responsible public policy would mandate the termination of pregnancy.

Advocates of a less than comprehensive ban may respond to the preceding arguments by pointing out that all legal bans function imperfectly. Although it is of course true that no law functions perfectly (eg, people continue to murder even though homicide is illegal), a society serious about prohibiting a certain act should adopt laws that will reduce, to the greatest extent possible, the likelihood of that act occurring. Although a comprehensive ban on human cloning may indeed fail to prevent all instances of reproductive cloning, prohibiting not only the implantation but also the creation of cloned human embryos would prove to be a far more effective mechanism for securing a society free from reproductive cloning. A comprehensive cloning ban is also the only policy consistent with the priority medicine should place on the value of human life. . . .

Legal and Ethical Precedent

Although a strong lobby to legalize research cloning has been formed by certain scientist, biotechnology firms, and patient advocacy groups, the fact remains that the prospect of creating and destroying human embryos for research purposes has, for valid reasons, been consistently opposed in both the legal and the ethical arenas. It is incumbent on advocates of research cloning who wish to overturn well-established ethical standards to make and defend a sufficient and compelling case. No convincing case has been presented that provides substantive arguments for rejecting the existing set of governing principles that has been carefully formulated and deeply etched into the prevailing ethos of our culture.

A policy allowing research cloning would therefore run counter to US jurisprudence regarding the treatment of human embryos and to the intent of ethical codes designed to protect human subjects in research. Of note, a noncomprehensive ban permitting research cloning would establish, for the first time in US history, a class of human beings created for the sole purpose of experiments that will destroy them and whom ironically it is a crime *not* to destroy. In recognition of this fact, and of research cloning's inherent potential for reproductive applications, the burden of proof must lie on those who wish to justify such a momentous break with legal and ethical precedent. We assert that no such justification has been offered. . . .

"First, Do No Harm"

Considered realistically, human cloning fails to qualify as a healing act. The physician's integrity as a healer requires that he or she always act to preserve life, and never by means of human death. The intention to heal can in no way justify the act of terminating the life of another human being. Accordingly, physicians consider nonmaleficence to be a more stringent ethical obligation than beneficence. Such ordering of ethical priorities in medicine has long placed the profession of medicine on higher moral ground than that reachable by pragmatic rationalizations. This is why Hippocrates' prime maxim, "First, do no harm," has endured since antiquity as a guiding principle among physicians who, by honoring it, have earned their patients' trust.

To rewrite medical ethics to permit human cloning would ensnare physicians in a perilous compromise of professional standards. To acquiesce to human embryonic cloning would be to disregard, to an unprecedented degree, the value of new human life. Human cloning would also represent a decided step toward the devaluing of humanity universally because justifications of human cloning research disturbingly imagine a category of dismissable human life. Such a designation is utterly foreign to the Hippocratic ethic, which respects human beings at all stages of life.

Although the potential for eventual health benefits from research cloning has been vigorously advanced, its violation of human dignity by treating nascent human life as no more valuable than an expendable means to others' ends falls short of the purpose for which medicine exists. The medical good aims not only to improve physiologic function and to secure the good as perceived by the patient but also strives to safeguard and promote the higher good for the patient. This higher good includes the preservation of the dignity of humans as humans, for which the physician is obligated to guard the welfare of the most vulnerable of human beings, including the cloned human embryo.

All Forms of Cloning Should Be Banned

Human cloning, for whatever purpose, represents an abuse of scientific freedom, not its realization. This new technology should adhere to the standard that science should always serve humanity, never that a segment of humanity would be created to serve science. As history has conspicuously recorded, no program sacrificing those at the margins of humanity to science has ever stood the test of time. Ethical reflection always reaches, in due course, the conclusion that the least of human beings deserve the care and concern that the medical profession presumes is due all human beings. Whether the ethical cinder of human cloning will lodge in the eye of society's conscience is an issue still within the reach of sensible preventive intervention.

For the sake of their patients, as well as the future of humanity, we urge health care professionals to oppose all forms of human cloning. In keeping with the Hippocratic ethic, we recommend that biomedical research on non-embryonic stem cells be pursued and funded aggressively. We also commend legislation and policies at all levels that will protect people from the unfavorable outcomes of human cloning, both now and for generations to come. Only a ban prohibiting both research and reproductive cloning will offer such protection.

> *"The mere fact that an area of research appears to offend a particular social convention or world view is, in general, not enough to justify government interference with that research activity."*

A Ban on Cloning Research Cannot Be Justified

Timothy Caulfield

Timothy Caulfield argues in the following viewpoint that it is difficult to defend a complete ban on cloning. He maintains that the right to freedom of expression protects scientific cloning research. According to Caulfield, the moral status of the embryo guides much of the argument against cloning. However, not all religions agree that human life begins at conception. A ban on scientific research that is based on contested moral values simply cannot be justified when other, less restrictive measures are available. Caulfield is the research director of the Health Law Institute at the University of Alberta in Edmonton, Canada.

As you read, consider the following questions:

1. According to the Canadian Supreme Court, as cited by Caulfield, what is one of the rationales for protecting freedom of expression?
2. What is one of the specific social goals of academic freedom, in Caulfield's opinion?
3. What percentage of Canadians support a complete ban on human cloning, as cited by the author?

[In 2004], the Canadian government enacted the Assisted Human Reproduction Act. The new law, which is likely to come into force in the near future, creates a useful regulatory scheme that will oversee all clinical and research activities involving human reproductive material. However, the law also criminally prohibits certain activities, including research cloning. As in many countries, research cloning—also known as therapeutic or non-reproductive human cloning—has been a focus of public debate.

Scientific Freedom

Although the long-term clinical value of this promising area of research is far from established, the banning of research cloning stands as a good example of the challenges associated with the regulation of scientific activities that engage contested social values. For example, the ban forces us to consider when it is appropriate for a government to interfere with scientific freedom.

In the USA, several commentators have argued that the scientific work of researchers enjoys protection under the First Amendment of the American Bill of Rights. [M.K.] Cantrell suggests: "There is domestic case law and international precedent to support scientists' freedom of scientific inquiry. At least in the US, a complete ban on [cloning] research would face an uphill constitutional battle in the courts." In Canada, there are grounds to support the view that the new ban may breach the Canadian Charter of Rights and Freedoms. Although there are no cases directly about this point, the Canadian Supreme Court has noted that one of the specific rationales for protecting freedom of expression is "the benefits to be gained from the pursuit of truth and creativity in science, art, industry and other endeavours". Worldwide, the 1966 International Covenant on Economic, Social and Cultural Rights compels treaty countries to respect the freedom necessary for scientific research.

Not all, however, are convinced that scientific freedom is a legally protected social norm. A recent report by the President's Council on Bioethics, for instance, largely discounts scientific freedom as an over-riding legal right. But even if one does not agree that scientific freedom is protected by human rights and national constitutional law, it is hard to completely dismiss its relevance to policy development. Few would argue that governments can arbitrarily dictate how research can be done. In universities, for example, the closely related concept of academic freedom is a widely accepted guiding principle. And one of the specific social goals of academic freedom is to protect against ideological interference with scholarly activity. The mere fact that an area of research appears to offend a particular social convention or world view is, in general, not enough to justify government interference with that research activity.

From the jailing of Galileo to the Scopes trial on the teaching of evolution, there are countless cautionary tales that highlight the perils of allowing any single ideological view to dominate science policy. At a minimum, the concept of scientific freedom serves as a lens through which to view the legitimacy of a given regulatory approach. It places the onus of justification on those seeking to curtail scientific inquiry and should force us to consider whether there are other, less intrusive, regulatory instruments that could be used to achieve the policy objectives.

A Complete Ban Is Hard to Defend

For many, myself included, a complete prohibition of research cloning seems hard to defend. Indeed it has been suggested that such bans represent an unprecedented interference by government in scientific and academic inquiry. This reaction is partly based on the reality that the desire for a ban appears to be motivated by a particular view of the moral status of the fetus.

In Canada, for example, abortion politics dominated much of the Parliamentary debate about cloning. In the USA, abortion remains the single biggest factor in the development of stem-cell policy. Even in the UK [United Kingdom] which has one of the most sophisticated regulatory systems, prolife rhetoric has had an important role in the evolution of policy.

But it must not be forgotten that there remains no consensus on the moral status of the embryo. Islamic and Jewish positions differ greatly from the traditional Catholic view that the embryo has moral status upon conception. Even within the Christian faith there is diversity of opinion. Additionally, there is little evidence of consensus among the general public. For instance, despite the Canadian Government's decision to ban research cloning, all the evidence indicates that the public supports the activity. A 2002 poll found that six in ten Canadians approve of the creation of cloned human embryos for collecting stem cells. Another study found that 21% oppose any law that restricts research into human cloning; 39% support a ban on human cloning, while allowing research on cloned embryos; and only 33% support a complete ban on all human cloning.

In countries with a homogeneous religious perspective that is an accepted part of the political system, a faith-based approach to science policy may, at least from a national perspective, be tolerable. But in liberal democracies that have embraced a more pluralistic view of society, such an approach is untenable—particularly when viewed through the lens of scientific freedom. As noted by [J.] Childress in relation to US stem-cell policy: "An ethical public policy in our pluralistic society has to respect diverse fundamental beliefs. And yet it must not be held hostage to any single view of embryonic life."

Other Justifications

Of course, concern about the moral status of the fetus is not the only rationale used to justify a ban on research cloning. Concern about the commodification of human reproductive material and slippery-slope arguments pervade much of the policy discussions. However, in most countries, these issues have not had the same political currency as concerns about the moral status of the embryo. Also, it seems possible to address these concerns with regulatory strategies that can respect scientific freedom by being less restrictive than an outright ban. For example, the commodification concern could be addressed by regulating the buying and selling of human reproductive material. There is a good deal of precedent for such an approach. Kidney transplantation promotes the commodification of human tissue, but we do not ban transplantation, we ban the buying and selling of organs. Similarly, the slippery-slope concern (rarely a good rationale for a law) could be addressed by banning the feared activity—in this case, reproductive cloning. Again, this approach accords with existing science policy. We do not ban research involving dangerous chemicals, atomic energy, and addictive drugs, we regulate their use.

A Virtual Ban

[George W. Bush's] "limited" federal research results in a virtual ban on useful stem cell research. . . .

As Princeton University President Shirley M. Tilghman, a professor of molecular biology, noted . . . , "Unless something is done, a promising area of biomedical research with potential for curing diseases like juvenile diabetes and Parkinson's will be curtailed, and the United States will be at a serious competitive disadvantage with other countries that are actively pursuing this research.". . .

Why should our national policy force our best scientists to spend years researching a way to clean-up contaminated stem cells when other stem cells exist that can advance scientific knowledge today? . . .

I want this country's scientists spending their time finding cures to horrible diseases—not trying to work through a virtual ban on their research.

Richard J. Codey, letter to President George W. Bush, January 25, 2005.

Regardless of the strength of its legal status, scientific freedom clearly has limits. Obviously, the safety and respect of research participants takes precedence over any research agenda. Indeed, the Helsinki Declaration here emphasises that "[i]n medical research on human subjects, considerations related to the well-being of the human subject should take precedence over the interests of science and society". However, in the context of research cloning, the application of this widely accepted principle depends greatly on the moral status of the embryo. Even the President's Council on Bioethics concedes that the relevance of scientific freedom to the regulation of stem-cell research largely "turns on the status of the extra-uterine human embryos".

A Ban Cannot Be Justified

In a world where science policy is increasingly influenced by politics, economics, and religion, the concept of scientific freedom has never been more important. Whilst there is no doubt that controversial research should be subject to reasonable regulatory oversight, a principled justification for the nature of the regulatory approach must be provided. A justification based primarily on a contested social value, such as the moral status of the fetus, is simply insufficient—particularly when the chosen regulatory instrument is a criminal ban, the most restrictive regulatory tool available. As nicely summarised by [C.] Shalev: "The moral status of the embryo is a cultural issue on which even religions may differ and is therefore not sufficient justification to ban cloning."

"Reproductive cloning is not a solution to problems such as infertility; we already have better means of achieving that goal. Nor is it a medical treatment."

Reproductive Cloning Should Be Banned

Atlanta Journal-Constitution

The editors of the *Atlanta Journal-Constitution* contend in the following viewpoint that reproductive cloning should be banned, while therapeutic cloning should be allowed to continue. They argue that there are other and better means of treating infertility than reproductive cloning. On the other hand, therapeutic cloning could potentially lead to treatments for many serious diseases and injuries. Many countries have embraced therapeutic cloning research and treatments, the editors maintain. If the United States were to ban therapeutic cloning, researchers would simply move to another country that allows it.

As you read, consider the following questions:

1. What announcement reignited a debate about the merits of human cloning, according to the authors?
2. What are some of the motives attributed to those who want to replicate a specific individual, in the authors' opinion?
3. What scientific development of the twentieth century do the authors equate cloning with?

The challenges that confronted this nation prior to Sept. 11 [2001] have begun to reassert themselves, demanding that attention be paid. None of those issues will be more difficult, or in the end more important, than the debate about human cloning.

[In November 2001], a Massachusetts company reignited the discussion by announcing that it had attempted to create human clones for purposes of medical research. In scientific terms, the work by Advanced Cell Technology broke little new ground. But it did represent a bold declaration of intent by the company, one of the more aggressive players in the biotechnology field.

And it certainly drew the attention of politicians.

"I believe it will be perhaps a big debate," Sen. Richard Shelby (R-Ala.) said. "But at the end of the day, I don't believe that we're going to let the cloning of human embryos go on." President [George W.] Bush also reiterated his opposition to the practice.

What Is Needed

As Shelby suggests, we need a thoughtful, well-informed and broadly based debate about the implications of human cloning, with the probable goal of outlawing some uses of the technique altogether. And we need that discussion soon.

As the ACT announcement indicates, delaying the debate any longer would be foolhardy. If we refuse to address this issue head-on, we merely cede the decision to scientists and business people who have neither the training nor the obligation to consider broader issues.

The discussion must begin by making a distinction about goals. The ACT research, like most of the other mainstream work on human cloning, is a form of medical research. In simple terms, scientists take an unfertilized human egg and remove its genetic content. They then inject the empty egg with the contents of a skin cell or other cell taken from a living person. The egg, not "programmed" with a full set of genetic data, begins to divide just as a normal embryo would.

Ideally, in a few days the dividing egg produces stem cells that are identical in genetic makeup to the patient who donated the initial cell. Those stem cells could then be used to produce tissue to treat that patient for a range of human illnesses from diabetes to Alzheimer's disease.

Human Cloning

The second, and more lurid, goal of human cloning is to create a genetic duplicate of a living human being. The initial technique is much the same as with therapeutic cloning. However, once the vacated egg is fertilized with the contents of a living cell, it is implanted in a human womb and allowed to develop into a baby.

There are no larger social goals at stake in that second process. Reproductive cloning is not a solution to problems such as infertility; we already have better means of achieving that goal. Nor is it a medical treatment. Those who wish to use the technique to replicate a specific individual have motives ranging from the vainly sentimental (they want to reproduce a loved one) to the egotistic (they want to reproduce themselves) to the downright diabolical.

Anderson. © by Kirk Anderson. Reproduced by permission

Weighing the meager benefits of human reproductive cloning against its risks, the verdict seems clear: Cloning for purposes of human reproduction ought to be banned, not merely by the United States but through an international agreement binding on all civilized nations. Perhaps the prospect of becoming international criminals ostracized by the scientific community would be enough to dissuade researchers who might otherwise be tempted to defy the ban.

A Grave Step

In advocating that step, it's important to acknowledge the gravity of what we're doing. Western society has seldom tried to outlaw any form of scientific research or experimentation. In those rare cases when governments did try to intervene in science, the verdict of history has not been kind.

Leonardo da Vinci, for example, had to keep his notebooks on human anatomy secret, because at the time the dissection of human corpses was considered a sacrilege, just as many people today are repulsed by the idea of cloning. Copernicus, Galileo and others risked excommunication and even death to spread what they learned about the sun and planets.

It is possible that our descendants will someday look at a ban on reproductive cloning much as we view the ban on dissection during da Vinci's time. To them, it may seem a quaint and hopeless gesture against the technological imperative that what can be, will be.

However, it seems equally plausible that our descendants will embrace a ban on reproductive cloning as proper and necessary. Times have changed. With the atomic bomb, science for the first time gave us a tool that we are not equipped to handle. Cloning for reproductive purposes falls into that category, as well. On rare occasions—and they will come more often now—we must be prepared to say "no" to what science offers.

Impossible, Immoral, and Impractical

The debate over cloning as a medical technique is much more complicated, however. It seems impossible and perhaps even immoral to try to ban an approach with so much promise for treating so many human illnesses. Dying patients and their loved ones are simply not going to accept a law that puts a potential cure out of their reach, and it's hard to argue that they should.

Furthermore, the international consensus that makes possible a ban on reproductive cloning does not exist on therapeutic cloning. As a practical matter, if we ban the technique here in the United States, research will simply move to Britain and other nations that have already embraced it.

Congress can, and should, ban cloning as a means to replicate individual human beings. But banning it as a means of saving lives is simply not possible.

"A ban would prevent people from making choices aimed at improving their lives that would hurt no one."

Reproductive Cloning Should Not Be Banned

Gregory Stock

In the following viewpoint Gregory Stock argues that it is wrong to ban human reproductive cloning. He maintains that the policies necessary to block human cloning would be so intrusive and so harsh that they would cause greater harm to society than the technology itself. Cloning a human hurts no one, Stock maintains, and while the new technology will present challenges, society can face those problems when they arise. Stock is the director of the Program of Medicine, Technology, and Society at the University of California at Los Angeles School of Medicine. He is also the author of *Redesigning Humans: Our Inevitable Genetic Future*.

As you read, consider the following questions:

1. How would banning biomedical technology serve to foster deep class divisions, in the author's view?
2. What is Stock's response to those who argue that parents will begin to choose embryos if the technology is allowed?

There has been a lot of hand wringing recently about cloning. Considering that not a single viable cloned human embryo has yet been created, that the arrival of a clinical procedure to do so seems quite distant, and that having a delayed identical twin (which is, after all, what a clone is) has limited appeal, why all the fuss?

No Law Can Stop New Technology

The fuss arises because cloning has become a proxy for broader fears about the new technologies emerging from our unraveling of human biology. Critics like Francis Fukuyama imagine that if we can stop cloning we can head off possibilities like human enhancement [via genetic engineering], but they're dreaming. As we decipher our biology and learn to modify it, we are learning to modify ourselves—and we will do so. No laws will stop this.

Embryo selection[1], for example, is a mere spin-off widely supported medical research of a sort that leaves no trail and is feasible in thousands of labs throughout the world. Any serious attempt to block such research will simply increase the potential dangers of upcoming technologies by driving the work out of sight, blinding us to early indications of any medical or social problems.

A Ban Would Be Wrong

The best reason not to curb interventions that many people see as safe and beneficial, however, is not that such a ban would be dangerous but that it would be wrong. A ban would prevent people from making choices aimed at improving their lives that would hurt no one. Such choices should be allowed. It is hard for me to see how a society that pushes us to stay healthy and vital could justify, for instance, trying to stop people from undergoing a genetic therapy or consuming a drug cocktail aimed at retarding aging. Imposing such a ban requires far more compelling logic than the assertion that we should not play God or that, as Fukuyama has suggested, it is wrong to try to transcend a "natural" human life span.

1. Embryo selection involves creating embryos outside the womb and testing their genetic characteristics prior to implantation in the womb.

What's more, a serious effort to block beneficial technologies that might change our natures would require policies so harsh and intrusive that they would cause far greater harm than is feared from the technologies themselves. If the War on Drugs, with its vast resources and sad results, has been unable to block people's access to deleterious substances, the government has no hope of withholding access to technologies that many regard as beneficial. It would be a huge mistake to start down this path, because even without aggressive enforcement, such bans would effectively reserve the technologies for the affluent and privileged. When abortion was illegal in various states, the rich did not suffer; they just traveled to more-permissive locales.

A Constitutional Right to Reproduce

The Supreme Court has ruled that every American has a constitutional right to "bear or beget" children. This includes the right of infertile people to use sophisticated medical technologies like in vitro fertilization.

[But] a *Consumer Reports* study concludes that fertility clinics produce babies for only 25 percent of patients. That leaves millions of people who still cannot have children, often because they can't produce viable eggs or sperm, even with fertility drugs. Until recently, their only options have been to adopt or to use eggs or sperm donated by strangers.

Once cloning technology is perfected, however, infertile individuals will no longer need viable eggs or sperm to conceive their own genetic children—any body cell will do. Thus, cloning may soon offer many Americans the only way possible to exercise their constitutional right to reproduce. For them, cloning bans are the practical equivalent of forced sterilization.

Mark D. Eibert, *Reason*, June 1998.

Restricting emerging technologies for screening embryos would feed deep class divisions. Laboratories can now screen a six-cell human embryo by teasing out a single cell, reading its genes, and letting parents use the results to decide whether to implant or discard the embryo. In Germany such screening is criminal. But this doesn't deny the technology to affluent Germans who want it: They take a trip to Brussels or London, where it is legal. As such screenings become easier and more informative, genetic disease could be gradually relegated to society's disadvantaged. We need to start thinking about how to make the tests more, not less, accessible.

But let's cut to the chase. If parents can easily and safely choose embryos, won't they pick ones with predispositions toward various talents and temperaments, or even enhanced performance? Of course. It is too intrusive to have the government second-guessing such decisions. British prohibitions of innocuous choices like the sex of a child are a good example of undesirable government intrusion. Letting parents who strongly desire a girl (or boy) be sure to have one neither injures the resulting child nor causes gender imbalances in Western countries.

Sure, a few interventions will arise that virtually everyone would find troubling, but we can wait until actual problems appear before moving to control them. These coming reproductive technologies are not like nuclear weapons, which can suddenly vaporize large numbers of innocent bystanders. We have the luxury of feeling our way forward, seeing what problems develop, and carefully responding to them.

The Real Danger

The real danger we face today is not that new biological technologies will occasionally cause injury but that opponents will use vague, abstract threats to our values to justify unwarranted political incursions that delay the medical advances growing out of today's basic research. If, out of concern over cloning, the U.S. Congress succeeds in criminalizing embryonic stem cell research that might bring treatments for Alzheimer's disease or diabetes—and Fukuyama lent his name to a petition supporting such laws—there would be real victims; present and future sufferers from those diseases.

We should hasten medical research, not stop it. We are devoting massive resources to the life sciences not out of idle curiosity but in an effort to penetrate our biology and learn to use this knowledge to better our lives. We should press ahead. Of course, the resultant technologies will pose challenges: They stand to revolutionize health care and medicine, transform great swaths of our economy, alter the way we conceive our children, change the way we manage our moods, and even extend our life spans.

The possibilities now emerging will force us to confront the question of what it means to be a human being. But however uneasy these new technologies make us, if we wish to continue to lead the way in shaping the human future we must actively explore them. The challenging question facing us is: Do we have the courage to continue to embrace the possibilities ahead, or will we succumb to our fears and draw back, leaving this exploration to braver souls in other regions of the world?

"That which can be done in medical technology will ultimately be done somewhere sometime by someone. Cloning is no exception."

Laws Will Not Prevent Human Cloning

A. James Rudin

In early 2003, the Raelians—a religious sect that claims extraterrestrials created human life on Earth—announced that a biotechnology company founded by its followers had cloned the first human baby, whom they called Eve. In the following viewpoint A. James Rudin explains that the announcement prompted leading political and religious leaders to denounce human cloning and the U.S. Congress to propose legislation to ban the technology. Rudin contends that a ban on human cloning is worthless because if the technology exists, it will eventually be done somewhere. Rudin, a rabbi and visiting professor at St. Leo University in Florida, is the senior interreligious adviser at the American Jewish Committee in New York City.

As you read, consider the following questions:

1. Who is Eve's mother, according to Rudin?
2. According to the author, why did Eve's mother give birth outside the United States?
3. What are the questions about cloning that Rudin says must be faced?

A. James Rudin, "Raelian Cloning Claim Obscures Real Challenges," *National Catholic Reporter*, January 17, 2003. Copyright © 2003 by the National Catholic Reporter, www.natcath.org. Reproduced by permission.

It's too bad the serious bioethical questions of human cloning got enmeshed with the Raelians, a wacky religious sect that focuses on aliens and promises eternal life by "downloading" our personal memory banks and unique personalities into other human beings.

It's too bad because cloning, not the clowning of cult leader Claude Varilhon, AKA Rael, presents profound religious, political and scientific challenges our society must address.

The Birth of a Clone?

Unfortunately, the recent bizarre news conference in Florida didn't advance a thoughtful cloning debate. Chemist Brigitte Boisselier, a Raelian bishop and an official of Clonaid, allegedly a separate corporate entity from the Raelians, proudly announced the birth of Eve, the world's first successfully cloned human. The mother is said to be a 31-year-old American, but Eve's birth took place outside the United States to avoid possible civil or criminal lawsuits.

As of this writing, no Baby Eve has been presented to a skeptical world, and news reports say the cloned child will be kept from public view until she is 18 years old. Such foolishness provides an easy target for harsh criticism—one of Israel's leading rabbis, the pope and the presidents of the United States and France wasted no time in denouncing the cloning of humans.

Several congressional leaders immediately followed the American custom of demanding new restrictive laws whenever something unknown, threatening or unpopular emerges. The House of Representatives has already adopted legislation banning all forms of cloning, but the measure failed to pass in the Senate because a bipartisan group led by Sens. Orrin Hatch, R-Utah, Arlen Specter, R-Pa., Dianne Feinstein, D-Calif., and Edward Kennedy, D-Mass., spoke in favor of therapeutic cloning, something quite distinct from the reproductive cloning claimed by the Raelians.

The senators do not want to close off the possibility of producing not new humans but fresh embryonic stem cells that can be used for medical research in combating diabetes, Parkinson's disease and ALS (Lou Gehrig's disease), among other illnesses. . . .

Time to Get Serious

Because there is much more to cloning than a white robed cult leader from France and his bishop who once taught chemistry, it's time to follow the lead of the four senators and get serious.

I am a member of the New York State Task Force on Life and the Law, a group of 25 clergy, physicians, lawyers, hospital administrators, nurses, ethicists and social workers who have been drafting proposed bioethical legislation since 1985 on such issues as organ transplants, assisted suicide, surrogate parenting, prenatal testing, withdrawal and withholding of life support systems, and a host of other questions involving patients' rights.

THE GENIE OUT OF THE BOTTLE...

Shelton. © 1998 by King Features Syndicate. Reproduced by permission.

My task force work has taught me one indelible lesson: That which can be done in medical technology will ultimately be done somewhere sometime by someone.

Cloning is no exception. If Rael and his merry band of 55,000 members in 84 countries don't successfully perform human cloning, someone else will and it will be sooner rather than later; not if but when.

Remember the joke about three people living on a tiny

tropical island that is about to be covered by a gigantic tidal wave? One person responds by praying the massive storm will bypass the island. The second person sends out an SOS distress call on the radio. The third person, as the tidal wave draws ever nearer, tells companions they have five minutes to learn how to survive under water.

Neither reproductive nor therapeutic cloning will be willed away by laws or prayers. There is no outside source to rescue society from this profound question. Despite the Raelians' insistence on extraterrestrial beings, it is we humans on Planet Earth who must learn to live with cloning in an ethical, compassionate and moral way.

Questions Must Be Answered

By resorting to political sloganeering and unexamined suppositions, we do ourselves and future generations a disservice. The questions are awesome, but they cannot be avoided.

Can therapeutic cloning combat the dread diseases many of us face? What are the theological implications of cloned humans? Will clones be burdened with severe psychological and physical disabilities? Will they be the "designer babies" of the rich and famous? Will they be clones or new humans created by an innovative technology not unlike in vitro reproduction or surrogate parenting? Are identical twins natural clones?

Be warned: The tidal wave of cloning is fast approaching.

"What [therapeutic cloning] offers today
. . . is a valuable addition to the scientific
toolkit for understanding the process by
which an adult cell can regain some of its
youthful vigour."

Therapeutic Cloning Should Not Be Banned

Economist

Several infertility specialists have announced that they have cloned a human embryo and implanted it in a woman's womb. While there is no proof supporting any of these claims—or any resulting babies—many commentators have responded to the reports by calling for a ban on cloning. In the following selection, the editors of the *Economist*, a British publication, assert that due to the many risks involved, reproductive cloning should be banned. On the other hand, therapeutic cloning—which creates stem cells to be used to treat a wide variety of diseases—shows much promise and should remain legal.

As you read, consider the following questions:

1. According to the *Economist*, why do some people think reproductive cloning is wrong?
2. What is the one thing the United Nations has agreed upon concerning human cloning, according to the authors?
3. In the authors' opinion, what has blocked a global consensus on banning reproductive cloning?

Economist, "Pregnant Pause: Cloning," vol. 370, January 24, 2004, p. 13. Copyright © 2004 by The Economist Newspaper Ltd., www.economist.com. All rights reserved. Reproduced by permission.

Another year, another claim to fame through human cloning. On January 17th [2004], Panos Zavos, an American fertility specialist, announced to a press conference in London that he had managed to produce a human embryo through cloning, and then implanted it in a volunteer's womb.

At the moment, however, Dr Zavos seems strangely short of any sort of scientific evidence to back his claim. This is a common failing among those who seek the dubious distinction of being "the world's first human cloner". Severino Antinori, an Italian fertility doctor, also says he has produced several human clones, again without any proof. And . . . [in 2003], the world was agog with claims that the Raelians, a UFO-loving cult, had cloned a baby girl called Eve. Today the infant Eve is as elusive as her biblical namesake.

The Case Against Reproductive Cloning

Clearly, creating a human clone is hard. There are also many reasons why people think such reproductive cloning—creating an embryo by replacing the nucleus of an unfertilised egg with that of an adult cell, rather than allowing sperm and egg to meet—is wrong. Some are put off by the "unnatural" nature of the process. Others fear for the psychological welfare of a cloned child born, say, of a parent trying to recreate a dead relative. But there is also a clear scientific case against reproductive cloning. It remains dangerous for both mother and offspring. Cloned animals still perish in large numbers at all stages of development. If cloning were a drug, and not a procedure, no government in its right mind would allow it near the public given this abysmal safety record in animal testing.

While most countries have regulations on novel medicines, few have laws which deal explicitly with cutting-edge reproductive technology. The United Nations has spent the past three years trying to draft an international convention banning human cloning, but the only thing upon which the UN General Assembly has managed to agree is to discuss the issue again . . . [in 2004]. Member states are sharply divided between those, such as America, which want to ban all forms of human cloning and those, such as Britain, which want to allow one particular version of it, called therapeutic cloning.

Therapeutic Cloning

Therapeutic cloning involves the same laboratory procedure as reproductive cloning. Its aim, though, is not procreation but rather to create a source of so-called "stem cells", whose unusual properties make them a possible source of replacement tissue for a range of degenerative diseases. Those opposed to therapeutic cloning object to the creation—and destruction—of human life for such utilitarian ends. They argue that therapeutic cloning is unlikely to yield useful medical treatments, and fear the exploitation of women, particularly in poor countries, for their eggs. They also worry that therapeutic cloning opens the door to the reproductive variety.

An Absurd Position

If therapeutic cloning is recognised as potential benefit to patients, where no other curative remedies exist, it seems ethically questionable to block development of this technology based on a hypothetical misuse of that technology. Generalising such a position to other areas of medicine one would quickly end in absurdity. It would clearly be unethical to abstain from treating a heart patient with digitalis based on the fear that somebody else might use digitalis as a deadly poison. If reproductive cloning should not be allowed to happen, then that is what should be prohibited. Specifically this would require prohibition of implantation in a female uterus of a transnuclear egg cell.

J-E. S. Hansen, *Journal of Medical Ethics*, April 2002.

But others want to give therapeutic cloning a chance. Although many Christians believe human life begins at conception, not all faiths agree and many people have no religious qualms. In any case, strong regulation and strict rules on egg donation can deal with some of these concerns. It is too early to tell if therapeutic cloning will transform medicine. What it offers today, however, is a valuable addition to the scientific toolkit for understanding the process by which an adult cell can regain some of its youthful vigour. If researchers knew enough to reproduce this effect with drugs, then they might be able to skip over embryonic stem-cells altogether, and move straight to stimulating adult cells already in the body.

America Should Moderate Its Stance

Disturbingly, opposition to all cloning, led by the United States, has in effect blocked a global agreement on banning the human-reproductive sort, even though nearly everyone agrees that this should be done, at least for now. America should moderate its all-or-nothing stance, help the UN move swiftly to approve a ban on reproductive cloning, and leave therapeutic cloning to the discretion of national governments.

In the meantime, countries should not use delays at the UN as an excuse to avoid passing their own national legislation. America, in particular, needs to put its house in order. Federal legislation on human-reproductive cloning has been held up in Congress for several years, again because of disagreement over whether to outlaw therapeutic cloning as well. Some states have passed their own laws, but such a piecemeal approach is unsatisfactory. America, like other nations, should act against reproductive cloning, and let scientists pursue the therapeutic variety. America's and the world's pregnant pause on cloning has lasted long enough.

Periodical Bibliography

The following articles have been selected to supplement the diverse views presented in this chapter.

Berit Brogaard   "The Moral Status of the Human Embryo: The Twinning Argument," *Free Inquiry*, Winter 2002.

Boston Globe   "Stem Cell Imperative," January 23, 2005.

Nell Boyce   "Is a Baby Clone on Board?" *U.S. News & World Report*, December 30, 2002.

Dennis Coday   "U.N. Abandons Cloning Ban," *National Catholic Reporter*, December 10, 2004.

Marcy Darnovsky   "Embryo Cloning and Beyond," *Tikkun*, July/August 2002.

Detroit Free Press   "Stem Cell Hope," January 12, 2005.

William A. Galston   "The Danger of Absolutes," *Public Interest*, Winter 2003.

Brian Harradine   "Beware the Push for Human Cloning," *Age*, July 31, 2004.

Richard Jerome   "Maybe Baby: History or Hoax?" *People Weekly*, January 13, 2003.

Stuart A. Newman   "Averting the Clone Age," *Journal of Contemporary Health Law and Policy*, Spring 2003.

Wendy Goldman Rohm   "Seven Days of Creation," *Wired*, January 2004.

Michael J. Sandel   "The Anti-Cloning Conundrum," *New York Times*, May 28, 2002.

Mary Ellen Schneider   "No Global Cloning Ban," *OB GYN News*, January 1, 2005.

Peter Singer   "The Harm That Religion Does," *Free Inquiry*, June/July 2004.

USA Today   "Stem Cell Policy Collapses," January 26, 2005.

Janet A. Warrington   "The Ethics of Reproductive Cloning," *Santa Clara Computer & High Technology Law Journal*, May 2003.

Jeff Wheelwright   "Being Brave for This New World," *Discover*, January 2003.

For Further Discussion

Chapter 1

1. Several authors assert that the terminology used to describe cloning techniques make a difference in how the procedures are viewed by society. For that reason, the President's Council on Bioethics chooses to use the terms "cloning-to-produce-children" instead of "reproductive cloning," and "cloning-for-biomedical-research" instead of "therapeutic cloning." Do you agree with the council and others who contend that the choice of terms can affect how questions are posed and answers are given? Why or why not?

2. Gregory E. Pence and others maintain that a clone is not an exact copy of its parent because a clone will have slightly different DNA due to the mitochondrial DNA of the egg cell and because the clone will not experience the same environment or have the same memories as its ancestor. Why do you suppose that some authors continue to invoke the image that cloning results in multiple, identical copies of an individual? In your opinion, is this an effective argument? Explain.

3. Wayne Pacella argues that cloning animals is immoral because there are millions of dogs and cats awaiting new homes in shelters and the supply of farm animals exceeds the demand for their meat, milk, and other products. He cites the case of a pet owner who spent $50,000 to clone a cat. Should the cost of the cloning procedure have any bearing on its morality? Why or why not?

Chapter 2

1. Ron Reagan, the son of President Ronald Reagan, who died after living with Alzheimer's disease for fifteen years, argues that embryonic stem cell research could lead to a cure for Alzheimer's disease. Wesley J. Smith contends, however, that embryonic stem cell research is wildly impractical and is unlikely to lead to effective treatments for diseases. These authors have distinctly different views about the effectiveness of therapeutic cloning. From your readings, which view is supported by more convincing evidence? Support your answer.

2. Jim Kelly cites genetic researcher Rudolf Jaenisha, who claims that reproductive cloning can never be safe because of the tendency of embryonic stem cells to form malignant tumors. How does Robert R. Rich respond to this argument? In your opinion, is using embryonic stem cells to treat diseases worth the risk? Explain.

Chapter 3

1. Steve Glassner maintains that embryonic stem cell research provides the most hope in repairing nerve damage in spinal cord injuries. Jean D. Peduzzi-Nelson argues, however, that adult stem cells are an effective treatment for spinal cord injuries. What evidence does each author present in support of the effectiveness (or lack thereof) of adult stem cells? Citing evidence from the viewpoints, explain whose argument is more persuasive.

2. Opponents of embryonic stem cell research contend that the embryo used in research is a viable human being that is killed during the course of research. Supporters of embryonic stem cell research maintain that the embryo used in research has only the potential to be human and is not yet a human being. Which view, in your opinion, is supported by more convincing evidence? Explain.

3. George Daley argues that while adult stem cells are a promising treatment for many diseases, they do not have the potential that embryonic stem cells have for curing many illnesses. Carolyn Moynihan contends that adult stem cells have been used successfully in treating diseases, while embryonic stem cells have not. Daley is a renowned biomedical scientist in stem cell research. Moynihan is a freelance journalist. Does knowing the authors' backgrounds influence your assessment of their arguments? Explain why or why not.

Chapter 4

1. The editors of the *Atlanta Journal-Constitution* argue that reproductive cloning is not a valid treatment for infertility. Gregory Stock contends that banning reproductive cloning would merely result in class divisions, since the rich would continue to find ways to clone themselves if they wanted. Whose argument is more persuasive, and why?

2. After reading all the viewpoints in this chapter, do you think all human cloning should be banned, that no human cloning should be banned, or that reproductive cloning should be banned while therapeutic cloning is allowed? Defend your answer with references to at least two viewpoints.

Organizations to Contact

Advanced Cell Technology
One Innovation Dr., Biotech Three, Worcester, MA 01605
(508) 756-1212 • fax: (508) 756-4468
Web site: www.advancedcell.com
Advanced Cell Technology, Inc., is a leading biotechnology company in the emerging field of regenerative medicine. Its focus is on cloning technology for the production of young cells for the treatment of cell degenerative diseases. Its Web site provides links to many scientific articles on cloning.

American Life League (ALL)
PO Box 1350, Stafford, VA 22555
(540) 659-4171 • fax: (540) 659-2586
e-mail: jbrown@all.org • Web site: www.all.org
ALL is an educational pro-life organization that opposes abortion, artificial contraception, reproductive technologies, and fetal experimentation. It asserts that it is immoral to perform experiments on living human embryos and fetuses, whether inside or outside the mother's womb. Its publications include the bimonthly magazine *Celebrate Life*, the fact sheet "Adult Stem Cell Research Successes," and the white paper "Broken Promises."

American Medical Association (AMA)
515 N. State St., Chicago, IL 60610
(800) 621-8335
Web site: www.ama-assn.org
The AMA is the largest and most prestigious professional association for medical doctors. It helps set standards for medical education and practices and is a powerful lobby in Washington for physicians' interests. The association publishes monthly journals for many medical fields as well as the weekly *JAMA* and the report *The Ethics of Cloning*.

American Society of Law, Medicine, and Ethics (ASLME)
765 Commonwealth Ave., Suite 1634, Boston, MA 02215
(617) 262-4990 • fax: (617) 437-7596
Web site: www.aslme.org
The society's members include physicians, attorneys, health-care administrators, and others interested in the relationship among law, medicine, and ethics. It takes no positions but acts as a forum for discussion of issues such as cloning. The organization has an

information clearinghouse and a library. It publishes the quarterlies *American Journal of Law* and *Journal of Law, Medicine, and Ethics*; the periodical ASLME Briefings; and books.

Americans to Ban Cloning (ABC)

Web site: www.cloninginformation.org

ABC is a coalition of organizations and individuals whose goal is to promote a comprehensive, global ban on cloning. Its members believe human cloning would commodify life and result in a race of second-class citizens. Its Web site offers a variety of articles, commentaries, and congressional testimony against human cloning.

Center for Bioethics and Human Dignity

2065 Half Day Rd. Bannockburn, IL 60015
(847) 317-8180 • fax: (847) 317-8101
e-mail: info@cbhd.org • Web site: www.cbhd.org

The Center for Bioethics and Human Dignity is an international education center whose purpose is to bring Christian perspectives to bear on contemporary bioethical challenges facing society. Its publications address human cloning and stem cell research as well as other topics in genetic technology. It publishes the newsletter *Dignity* and the policy statement "Human Cloning: The Need for a Comprehensive Ban."

Center for Biomedical Ethics

PO Box 33 UMHC, Minneapolis, MN 55455
(612) 625-4917
Web site: www.bioethics.umn.edu

The center seeks to advance and disseminate knowledge concerning ethical issues in health care and the life sciences. It conducts original research, offers educational programs, fosters public discussion and debate, and assists in the formulation of public policy. The center publishes the quarterly newsletter *Bioethics Examiner*, the monograph *Human Stem Cells*, and overviews on human cloning and stem cells.

Center for Genetics and Society

436 Fourteenth St., Suite 1302, Oakland, CA 94612
(510) 625-0819 • fax: (510) 625-0874
Web site: www.genetics-and-society.org

The Center for Genetics and Society is a nonprofit information and public affairs organization working to encourage responsible uses and effective societal governance of the new human genetic and reproductive technologies. Included among its publications are the newsletter *Genetic Crossroads* and the report *The New Technologies of Human Genetic Modification.*

Clonaid

Web site: www.clonaid.com

Clonaid was founded in 1997 by Raël, the spiritual leader of the Raelian Movement, the world's largest UFO-related organization. Clonaid is the first company to publicly announce its attempt to clone human beings. Clonaid believes that once human cloning has been perfected, the next step is to transfer memories and personalities into the newly cloned human brain, thus allowing a person to live forever. Clonaid and Raël have published the book *Yes to Human Cloning*, which examines why cloning is a feasible science.

Clone Rights United Front/Clone Rights Action Center

506 Hudson St., New York, NY 10014
(212) 255-1439 • fax: (212) 463-0435
e-mail: r.wicker@verizon.net • Web site: www.clonerights.org

The Clone Rights United Front was organized to oppose legislation that would make cloning a human being a felony. It is dedicated to the principle that reproductive rights, including cloning, are guaranteed by the Constitution, and that each citizen has the right to decide if, when, and how to reproduce. Its Web site has links to congressional testimony opposing a ban on human cloning and editorials supporting cloning.

Coalition for the Advancement of Medical Research (CAMR)

Web site: www.camradvocacy.org/fastaction

CAMR is comprised of nationally recognized patient organizations, universities, scientific societies, foundations, and individuals with life-threatening illnesses and disorders who advocate for the advancement of breakthrough research and technologies in regenerative medicine—including stem cell research and somatic cell nuclear transfer—in order to cure disease and alleviate suffering. The coalition believes embryonic stem cell research must remain a legal and protected form of scientific research. Its Web site offers a variety of links to press releases, editorials, and congressional testimony in support of its views.

The Genetics and Public Policy Center

1717 Massachusetts Ave. NW, Suite 530, Washington, DC 20036
(202) 663-5971 • fax: (202) 663-5992
e-mail: inquiries@DNApolicy.org
Web site: www.DNApolicy.org

The Genetics and Public Policy Center was established to provide information on genetic technologies and genetic policies to the public, media, and policy makers. The center undertakes public opinion polls concerning reproductive genetic technology. Its Web site includes the article *The Regulatory Environment for Human Cloning.*

Genetics Society of America
9650 Rockville Pike, Bethesda, MD 20814
(301) 571-1825 • fax: (301) 530-7079
Web site: www.genetics-gsa.org

The society is a professional organization of scientists and academics working in the field of genetic studies. It promotes the science of genetics and supports the education of students of all ages about the field. Its publications include the monthly journal *Genetics* and various educational materials on genetics.

The Hastings Center
21 Malcolm Gordon Rd., Garrison, NY 10524-5555
(845) 424-4040 • fax: (845) 424-4545
e-mail: mail@thehastingscenter.org
Web site: www.thehastingscenter.org

The center is a research institute that addresses fundamental ethical issues in health, medicine, and the environment, including issues related to genetics and human cloning. The center publishes books, papers, guidelines, and the bimonthly *Hastings Center Report*, which has published several articles on cloning.

Human Cloning Foundation
Web site: www.humancloning.org

The foundation promotes education, awareness, and research about human cloning and other forms of biotechnology. It emphasizes the positive aspects of these new technologies. The foundation prefers to distribute its information over the Internet and requests that people refrain from contacting it directly for information. Its Web site offers a variety of resources, including essays on the benefits of human cloning and an online newsletter, the *Cloner.*

Kennedy Institute of Ethics
Healy, 4th Fl., Georgetown University, Washington, DC 20057
(202) 687-8099 • fax: (202) 687-8089
Web site: www.georgetown.edu/research/kie

The institute sponsors research on medical ethics, including ethical issues surrounding the use of recombinant DNA and human gene therapy. It supplies the National Library of Medicine with an online database on bioethics and publishes an annual bibliography in addition to reports and articles on specific issues concerning medical ethics. The institute's publications include the quarterly journal *Kennedy Institute of Ethics Journal.* It also produces a series of papers that present overviews of issues and viewpoints related to particular topics in biomedical ethics.

National Institutes of Health (NIH)
9000 Rockville Pike, Bethesda, MD 20892
(301) 496-4000
Web site: http://stemcells.nih.gov

The NIH is the federal government's primary agency for the support of biomedical research. It is the government agency responsible for developing guidelines for research on stem cells. Its Web site includes numerous links to articles about stem cell research and frequently asked questions.

The President's Council on Bioethics (PCBE)
1801 Pennsylvania Ave. NW, Suite 700, Washington, DC 20006
(202) 296-4669
e-mail: info@bioethics.gov • Web site: www.bioethics.gov

The council was formed by an executive order in 2001 to advise the president on bioethical issues as a result of merging biotechnology. In addition, the council explores ethical and policy questions and provides a forum for a national discussion of these issues. Its reports include the books *Human Cloning and Human Dignity: An Ethical Inquiry* and *Being Human: Readings from the President's Council on Bioethics.*

The Reproductive Cloning Network
Web site: www.reproductivecloning.net

The Reproductive Cloning Network was established to store and review scientific resources regarding reproductive cloning. Its fundamental objective is to provide scientific information, statistics, and links to relevant companies and organizations. Its Web site provides a variety of links, articles, and resources about both human and animal cloning.

Bibliography of Books

Michael C. Brannigan, ed.	*Ethical Issue in Human Cloning: Cross-Disciplinary Perspectives.* New York: Seven Bridges, 2001.
Karl Drlica	*Understanding DNA and Gene Cloning: A Guide for the Curious.* Hoboken, NJ: Wiley, 2004.
Francis Fukuyama	*Our Post-Human Future: Consequences of the Biotechnology Revolution.* London: Profile, 2002.
Ronald Michael Green	*The Human Embryo Research Debates: Bioethics in the Vortex of Controversy.* New York: Oxford University Press, 2001.
John Harris	*On Cloning.* New York: Routledge, 2004.
Peter Michael Jack	*Thou Dust: A Philosophical Essay on Cloning.* Toronto: Timefoot Books, 2003.
Arlene Judith Klotzko, ed.	*The Cloning Sourcebook.* New York: Oxford University Press, 2001.
William Kristol and Eric Cohen, eds.	*The Future Is Now: America Confronts the New Genetics.* Lanham, MD: Rowman & Littlefield, 2002.
John Kunich	*The Naked Clone: How Cloning Bans Threaten Our Personal Rights.* Westport, CT: Praeger, 2003.
Paul Lauritzen, ed.	*Cloning and the Future of Human Embryo Research.* New York: Oxford University Press, 2001.
Stephen E. Levick	*Clone Being: Exploring the Psychological and Social Dimensions.* Lanham, MD: Rowman & Littlefield, 2004.
Jane Maienschein	*Whose View of Life? Embryos, Cloning, and Stem Cells.* Cambridge, MA: Harvard University Press, 2003.
Glenn McGee and Arthur Caplan, eds.	*The Human Cloning Debate.* Berkeley, CA: Berkeley Hills Books, 2004.
Sally Morgan	*Body Doubles: Cloning Plants and Animals.* Chicago: Heinemann Library, 2002.
Gregory E. Pence	*Cloning After Dolly: Who's Still Afraid of Human Cloning?* Lanham, MD: Rowman & Littlefield, 2004.
Gregory E. Pence	*Re-Creating Medicine: Ethical Issues at the Frontiers of Medicine.* Lanham, MD: Rowman & Littlefield, 2000.

Mark L. Perry

Frankenstein Is Alive! The Church's Position on Cloning. Cleveland Heights, OH: Geneva Books, 2001.

President's Council on Bioethics

Human Cloning and Human Dignity: An Ethical Inquiry. New York: PublicAffairs, 2002.

Stanley Shostak

Becoming Immortal: Combining Cloning and Stem-Cell Therapy. Albany: State University of New York Press, 2002.

Gregory Stock and John Campbell, eds.

Engineering the Human Germline: An Exploration of the Science and Ethics of Altering the Genes We Pass to Our Children. New York: Oxford University Press, 2000.

Claude Vorilhon

Yes to Human Cloning: Immortality Thanks to Science. Los Angeles: Tagman, 2001.

Brent Waters and Ronald Cole-Turner, eds.

God and the Embryo: Religious Voices on Stem Cells and Cloning. Washington, DC: Georgetown University Press, 2003.

Michael D. West

The Immortal Cell: One Scientist's Quest to Solve the Mystery of Human Aging. New York: Doubleday, 2003.

Index

stem cell research, and
curative potential of, 34, 51, 54, 87, 91
financial risk of, 84
juvenile diabetes and, 51, 56, 59, 62, 139
totipotent, 65
stem cell treatments and, 104, 106
dictators, cloning to create, 25
Discovery Institute, 58
diseases
adult stem cell treatments and, 104–108
autoimmune, 110
degenerative, 51, 59–60, 113, 157
in U.S. population, 88
see also genetic diseases
DNA, 14, 23, 51, 54, 69–70
Doerflinger, Richard M., 104
dogs, 14, 38
Dolly (sheep), cloning of, 10, 42
announcement of, 10–11, 14, 38, 123
Dolly-style embryos and, 48
intentions for, 11
Dominguez, Laura, 101–103
donor cells, 19, 32, 65, 69, 89, 94, 142
dopamine-producing cells, 54, 107

Economist (magazine), 155
Edinburgh, 42
Eibert, Mark D., 148
Eisenhower, Dwight D., 117
embryonic stem cell research (ESCR)
Catholic stance on, 111–13, 118
Christian stance on, 138, 157
criminalizing, 129, 149
financial aspects of, 84, 98, 111
Hippocratic ethic and, 133–34
impracticality of, 58–63
legal restrictions on, 84
loss of human life and, 29, 51, 82, 109–14, 116–17
pro-life support of, 94–95
saving human life and, 53–57, 79–80, 95
see also adult stem cell research, embryonic stem cell research and
embryonic stem cells
creation of
debates over, 31–32, 34, 54–55, 86, 89
economic advantages of, 111
federal funding and, 94
opponents of, 31–32, 112, 126, 128, 156
partial banning of, 129–32
supporters of, 34, 54–55, 138
unresolved issues concerning, 86,
88–89, 147
differentiating, 75, 77
flexibility of, 76, 79, 111
harvesting, 77
human life controversy and, 51–52, 77–79
plasticity of, 84
replication of, 55
tumor development and, 58
embryonic stem cell treatments, 34, 90–96, 104
embryos
aborted fetal tissue of, 84
of animals, 14
cloning process of, 34
discarded, 52, 59, 82, 92, 105, 120
frozen, 87, 95, 112, 116, 119–20
governmental policy to protect, 129
rights of, 31–32
SCNT-hES-1 and, 30–31
screening of, 148–49
Emory University School of Medicine, 64
endangered species, 10, 14, 42
environmental influences, on humans, 15, 23
Epstein, Alex, 33–36
eugenics, 21
European Journal of Neuroscience (magazine), 62
European Parliament, 87
euthanasia, 94
Eve (human clone), 151–52, 156
exotic animals, 10, 14

factory farms, 40
Fajt, John, 103
Fajt, Susan, 102–103
Family Research Council, 74
farmers, 39–40, 45–46
Faull, Richard, 83
FDA Consumer (magazine), 46
Federation of American Societies for Experimental Biology, 64, 67
Feinstein, Dianne, 152
fertility clinics, 87, 105, 130, 148
First Amendment, 136
Florida, 151–52
Florida Catholic Conference, 12
food, cloned, 39–40
Food and Drug Administration (FDA), 40–41, 46
food security, 37, 40, 46
foot-and-mouth disease, 40
Fox, Michael J., 91
France, 105, 152–53
Frankenstein (Shelley), 26
Fukuyama, Francis, 147

174